Praise for *Plastic-free*

'An excellent well-researched reference and the first book on how to reduce the use of plastics in horticulture. The author offers practical solutions to one of today's key environmental challenges for gardeners.'

Ken Cox, author of *Woodland Gardening, Garden Plants for Scotland, Fruit and Vegetables for Scotland*

'Author Fiona Thackeray's passion and talent for gardening shine through this comprehensive guide to dealing with the problem of plastic in our gardens.'

Claire Wingfield, author of *52 Dates for Writers* and rookie gardener

'Plastic use, recycling and avoidance, simply explained. A sensible and realistic guide to what you can do with a planned, staged approach to minimising the use of plastic in the garden. I want to buy a copy for all my gardening friends.'

Jan Cameron, author of *The Garden Cure*, publication summer 2020, Saraband

First published in Great Britain in 2019 by:

Trellis Books

Unit 8, 28 Glasgow Road

PERTH, PH2 0NX

A CIP catalogue record for this book is available from the British Library.

ISBN 978-1-9164919-0-8

Printed and bound in Great Britain by Bell & Bain Ltd.

Cover photography by Sharon Watters. Other photos: Sharon Watters and Fiona Thackeray.

PLASTIC-FREE GARDENING

A GUIDE TO REDUCING THE PLASTIC IN YOUR GARDENING LIFE

FIONA THACKERAY

ABOUT THE AUTHOR

Fiona Thackeray is the Head of Operations at Trellis, the therapeutic gardening charity for Scotland. She has worked in therapeutic gardening for 25 years, in the UK and overseas. In 2019 she received the Dr Andrew Duncan Medal for distinguished service to horticulture. She also writes novels and short fiction, for which she has won awards.

Find out more at www.fionathackeray.wordpress.com

ABOUT TRELLIS

Trellis supports therapeutic gardening groups, promotes gardening for wellbeing and helps people set up and develop programmes to share the powerful health benefits of gardening in hospitals, care homes, schools, prisons, hospices and community plots.

Find out more at www.trellisscotland.org.uk

CONTENTS

WHY BE A PLASTIC-FREE GARDENER?

When we think of plastic and the problems it causes, we don't often think of gardening. We think of beaches and riverbanks covered in debris and detritus. We think, perhaps, of the mess outside fast-food shops, in supermarket car parks, on pavements and motorway embankments and caught in the branches of trees in the park. I think of the wrapping that comes with me from the supermarket that I never intended to bring home, the little transparent box for a few pears, the surprise wrapping inside a box of tea, and I think of the unwelcome sight of plastic cups laid out beside a water jug when I go to a meeting.

But gardening seems like the kind of virtuous activity that must surely be almost free of plastic. A pure and timeless pursuit, rustic and noble, tending a haven unpolluted by plastic. Horticulture (encompassing the industry, the science and home gardening) has associations of craftsmanship and durability – tools of steel with turned ash handles, greenhouses built from glass and beech or aluminium, pots of terracotta and buckets made of zinc. That is how gardening seems to many of us who love it – until that is, we take a closer look.

When you next go into a garden, your own or one you're visiting, sweep your eyes over the materials there. From planters to power tools and plant labels, the chances are you'll see plenty of plastic in evidence. Next time you visit the garden centre, do a plastic audit: it's everywhere. Pots, of course, are the most obvious and prolific items, but there are plastic tools, plastic gloves, plastic fencing, cloches and other plastic coverings for crop protection like tunnels and fleece, and don't forget ground-cover membranes, plastic green-houses, ornaments and watering cans. Even the clothes we gardeners use often contain an awful lot of plastic.

Then there's the stealth plastic: the stuff you don't know you're buying, or that you buy unwittingly – even unwill-ingly – as part and parcel of something else. You set out to buy some rocket seeds and later when you open the packet, find it doesn't tear with the crisp rip of paper, but bends and stretches in the strange, shape-shifting way that only plastics do. Only then do you understand that the inside of the seed packet has been coated with a thin plastic layer. You pick up some compost, or manure, gravel or bark mulch, and are obliged to take home bags – of non-recyclable film – wrapped around your purchase. And when you buy plants, not only do you buy a plastic pot, but a little plastic name label too, and sometimes a plastic stake, just for good measure, only a few millimetres thick, but plastic, nevertheless, propping up your plant. Even most books contain plastic, though not, you will be glad to read, this one. These plastics, so abundant and various, are causing all sorts of havoc to our environment which we're only now beginning to understand better. It's a good time to stop and take stock; to develop a more conscious approach to our use of plastics.

In these chapters, we'll consider some of the effects of the plastic in our gardening lives, as well as some new technologies and ideas that promise to help tackle the problem. We'll look at the good things that gardeners and the horticulture trade are already doing to reduce plastic waste and of course there will be lots of ideas about how we gardeners can reduce our reliance on plastic.

At times, the scale of the plastic waste problem can seem overwhelming, too big for mere gardeners to tackle. But we shouldn't underestimate the power that lies in lots of people making one small change. Look at the recent revolutions that have come about through lots of individuals changing a tiny part of their routine. The plastic-bag tax, five pence on a single-use bag, led to millions of us refusing a bag a couple of times a week. The result: six billion bags saved in six months, a momentous 85% reduction. Later, a combination of tirelessly collected evidence and dedicated campaigning by ordinary people and more well-known folk stopped the use of microbeads in cosmetic products in 2018. Similar efforts to encourage whole cities and states to cut the use of plastic bottles and straws are already bearing fruit.

The UK is a nation of garden lovers, with half of all adults participating in some form of gardening, and we spend billions on this pastime every year. The impact, if we all make a small change in how we use plastic in the garden, will be phenomenal. And all the signs suggest that is exactly what's beginning to happen.

THE PROBLEM WITH PLASTIC

Of course, plastic is fantastic. It doesn't leak, it contains and isolates substances that may otherwise be smelly or toxic or stain our clothes, our cars, our skin. It's strong, lightweight and malleable, able to morph into all kinds of shapes, and it's washable, we can clean it very easily. Finally, it has impressive durability, that most double-edged of plastic's qualities. These many desirable properties go some way to explaining why we fell for plastic so hard and find ourselves surrounded by the stuff today.

In the 1967 film, *The Graduate*, Mr McGuire (played by Walter Brooke) says, rather enigmatically, to a young Dustin Hoffman at his 'Homecoming' party, "I want to say one word to you, just one word. Plastics ... There's a great future in plastics." While there may be other threads to this scene, it certainly expresses the feeling of the era that plastics were a modern wonder product offering huge potential. The year after the film's release saw a huge boom for plastic manufacturing for which many people credit McGuire's line. Brooke once told his nephew that he'd have invested in plastics himself, if he'd known the remark might prefigure such success.

Earlier still, in *It's a Wonderful Life*, Sam Wainwright offers James Stewart's George Bailey a bright future in plastics, "... It's gonna make us all rich ... the chance of a lifetime". When George prevaricates rather than grabbing a slice of the action, Sam suggests he's a bit of a loser, saying, "Unless you're still married to that broken-down building and loan. It's the biggest thing since radio and I'm lettin' you in on the ground floor." During WWII, Wainwright does indeed make a fortune manufacturing plastic hoods for aeroplanes.

Plastics have been used for lots of incredible medical innovations like prosthetic limbs, colostomy bags, heart pumps and stents, syringes and the safe containment and disposal of blades and needles. They have been used to improve hygiene, to create inspiring toys for children, safety-enhancing car parts, beautiful art and all manner of lightweight industrial parts. Plastics truly are an innovation that human beings can be proud of. The problem lies, to a large degree, in their after-life, their permanence after we have no more use for them, and their abundance. We've become so addicted to their convenience that we've turned to them to solve our problems in every area of life – and come to rely on them.

Plastics are a class of substances called polymers, whose long-chained molecular structures are created by fusing together substances with short molecular chains, a process called polymerisation. Although there are polymers in nature, e.g. cellulose, the chains of molecules in synthetic polymers are often far longer. It is this molecular chain length that gives polymers the strength and flexibility we prize.

Plastics manufacturing relies heavily on our limited reserves of fossil fuels, both for raw materials and for the energy needed to process them. And where fossil fuels are being consumed, it generally also implies certain amounts of pollution as a by-product. In addition, some plastics leach chemicals – such as Bisphenol A (BPA) – as they degrade, which can have harmful effects on wildlife and possibly human health. Worse, plastics marketed as biodegradable often have some accelerant ingredient added to speed their breaking down process, and that typically means additional polluting emissions concentrated over a shorter time frame.

Researchers from the University of Hawaii found that the

most common plastics release the greenhouse gases methane and ethylene as well as other chemicals harmful to the environment when sunlight exposure begins to degrade them. The amounts are described as 'traces' though they increase the more a plastic degrades, and plastic waste, considered in aggregate, is still a significant enough source of these gases to affect the climate. Plastic bags, as the world's most produced and discarded synthetic polymer, are the biggest source of such gas emissions from plastic. According to Friends of the Earth, producing these 'degradable' plastics with added accelerants does not help, on balance, with promoting sustainable plastic alternatives.

FROM GOOD INTENTIONS

The early plastics were developed in the 1800s, partly to relieve pressure on wildlife and the environment. Traditionally, buttons, handles, billiards balls and many other common objects were made from the shells of turtles and the horns of various animal species. So, developing a man-made substitute for these items would save the unnecessary exploitation of elephants, turtles, deer and other species for their ivory, horn and tortoiseshell. Today, with terrible irony, discarded plastic has become one of the biggest threats to wildlife, causing illness, disability and death for many creatures, and creating apparently intractable problems for our waterways and land habitats.

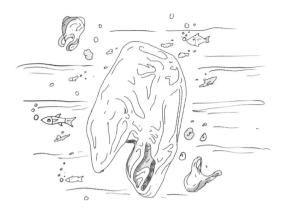

Plastic bags (particularly 'bunny bags', the ones whose handles look like rabbit ears) are easily mistaken for jellyfish, favourite food of turtles whose vision is not terribly sharp. The result, for a turtle, of ingesting a plastic bag is a slow death by malnutrition and drowning. A study from the Universities of Exeter and Plymouth, shared online by Sea Shepherd in January 2019 studied 102 sea turtles in three oceans and found every one of them had plastic in their bodies. Plastic rings used to hold beer cans and bottles together in packs of six can also be a plague on wildlife, causing strangulation for birds or trapping body parts in such an impossible position that the animals can't forage and feed or defend themselves and escape from prey.

In the BBC documentary *Drowning in Plastic*, presented by Liz Bonin (1 Oct 2018), viewers witnessed the tragic spectacle of flesh-footed shearwater chicks on Lord Howe Island with so many fragments of plastic in their stomachs that they were too heavy to lift off into flight. Shearwaters consume more plastic by weight than any other marine bird, and the chicks had 30–40 sharp, coin-sized pieces of plastic in their stomachs, including pieces of caps from drinks cartons and pen lids. This volume would be equivalent to a human eating ten kilograms of plastic. Apart from preventing them from foraging, these plastics, once lodged in the animals' bodies, are thought to interfere with hormone production and function.

In 2014 on an isolated beach on the northern coastline of Sao Paulo State, Brazil, I found a loggerhead sea turtle being pecked by vultures. Despite bringing the animal to a rescue centre in a nearby town, it died later that night. The cause? Plastic ingestion.

More recently, on 19 November 2018, a sperm whale washed up in Southeast Sulawesi, Indonesia, with a stomach full of plastic waste, nearly six kilograms of it, including 115 plastic cups. Turtles and other marine creatures falling victim to plastic – whether by ingestion or entrapment in fishing lines and nets – are now commonplace events: rescue organisations the world over deal with such cases routinely. The whale hit the headlines perhaps because, being such a big animal, it magnified the scale of the tragedy and so struck us more profoundly.

In reefs of the Asia–Pacific region, corals too are suffering from the plague of marine plastic, and some scientists think that the litter may also be acting as a vector of disease. Assistant Professor Joleah Lamb of the University of California, Irvine, has been studying the spread of a bacteria from the cholera family which she believes is being transmitted between corals in lethal doses by plastic waste. Plastic objects may create a wound on corals when they land, creating a channel for the microbes to enter and set about infecting the host organism. Seagrass meadows may play a role in trapping and disinfecting some of the plastic waste, and research effort will now focus on these crucial ecosystems.

Other unforeseen calamities arising from our plastic habit include the now famous microplastics. These are tiny fragments of plastic products that have begun to degrade but don't fully break down in the environment and instead persist as tiny particles that can be swallowed by animals at all levels of the food chain and so eventually, inevitably, could make it into human food. This is where, if it wasn't a worry already, the situation really begins to hit home for a lot of people. Microplastics, including microfibres, have been found in the Arctic, in walrus faeces and in plankton, several days' travel from Earth's most northerly human habitations. Nobody, not even the scientists studying microplastics, knows what these tiny remnants might do to the digestive systems and other vital bodily cycles of organisms of every size from microscopic plankton and fish to whales and humans.

Less well known and tinier still are nanoplastics, fragments smaller than a single algal cell. Scientists have begun to look at these more, but they are not so easy to isolate from water or earth samples as microplastics which can be strained out with filters. In theory, nanoplastics could absorb more pollutants and pass into more tissues and organs of animals and plants, or they may pass through harmlessly, but for now, very little indeed is understood about them.

There are other areas too, just as important to us as our food, where plastics have made the switch from wonder product to inconvenience to potential hazard. You may have heard of fatbergs, the disgusting phenomena that block up our public sewers. Pity the people who have to deal with these gruesome blockages straight out of a B-list sci-fi film.

Fatbergs are caused by an accumulation of fatty substances such as cooking fats and other grease mixed with wipes. You know – those convenient little napkin-like squares impregnated with cleaning fluids that can instantly swipe away any kind of mess from stickiness on fingertips to soapy gunk on sinks. Baby wipes, make-up removing wipes and household cleaning wipes have proliferated on supermarket shelves in recent years and found a snug niche in our car gloveboxes, bathroom cabinets and holiday luggage. These little swatches of cleanliness-restoring convenience typically contain – you guessed it – plastic. Although some wipes are plastic-free and claim to be flushable, they are generally made from a tough form of cellulose – a naturally occurring long-chain polymer – which is designed to withstand being soaked in fluids. They will still, therefore, take a long time to break up. The advice of experts from water companies and environmental specialists is to never flush wipes, even if they claim to be flushable (and, ideally, to reduce our use of them).

The labelling for some wipe products reminds us, in tiny apologetic font, not to flush them, but flush many people do. So, they end up floating and swooshing along waste pipes, meeting up with other wipes as they go.

Under the pavements of our cities they swim, sometimes snagging on a rough area of the sewer where the cement is not so smooth, or a tree root has penetrated. The flow at these spots gets more turbulent and snagged material is caught in a whirl, attracting other discarded wipes, congealed fat and various other, non-flushable, flushed materials such as sanitary towels, needles and cotton-bud stems. These compound into a growing protrusion with yet more non-biodegradable or slow-to-degrade materials. The whole snagging and swirling motion creates a snowball effect and the berg grows until it creates a blockage that can force drains to backup, posing a threat to human and animal health, causing great distress and incurring huge expense to the public purse in clean-up costs. Fatbergs can be as strong as concrete and require specialist companies to remove them.

Plastics appear in surprising guises. According to a report from NBC News, cigarette butts may be the single largest manmade contaminant of the oceans. When partially broken up, they also release the pollutants absorbed from tobacco smoke including arsenic, nicotine and lead. These can be consumed by sea creatures and can arrive back in our food chain: not everyone's favourite seasoning. Many people think of cigarette butts as being made of biodegradable natural fibre. They are made at least partly from cellulose acetate which certainly sounds natural, something similar to paper. But a non-biodegradable polymer often forms in the processing of this material, which explains why we often see cigarette filters that seem to hang around for years after being discarded. Cigarette butts make up a huge proportion of the litter collected from beaches; an estimated two thirds are not put in bins but discarded as litter. The most galling part is that filters are sold on a false promise: several studies have shown they don't make smoking any safer.

Globally, we buy one million plastic bottles every minute. We also buy a million disposable plastic cups and two million plastic bags. One truckload of plastic enters the ocean each minute, adding up to eight million every year. Another report suggests we produce 400 million tonnes of plastic worldwide each year, 40% of it single-use. In the Chitteram River in Indonesia, a raft of plastic waste over a mile long can arrive overnight in the middle of a riverside village after heavy rains. The plastic in these rafts stretches almost the entire width from bank to bank. The fishermen who once cast their nets and sold fish from these waters have given up and instead collect plastic to sell for recycling. Fish stocks in the Chitteram have fallen by 60%. In 2017, plastic waste was found at the bottom of the Mariana Trench, nearly seven miles down.

PLASTIC ISLAND

An island of plastic detritus in the middle of the ocean known as the Great Pacific Garbage Patch was recognised as a new state by UNESCO in 2013, following a request by an Italian artist hoping to raise awareness of the problem of plastic marine waste. The floating garbage patch is roughly halfway between Hawaii and California and although huge, it's not visible on satellite images because the debris is less densely packed than land masses and other structures recognisable from space. It's not even obvious to nearby people diving or in small boats because a lot of the debris is suspended microparticles and chemical sludge, which, while present in astoundingly high densities, is not always very clear to the human eye.

The debris in the Garbage Patch is trapped by current patterns of the North Pacific Gyre that is thought to gradually concentrate marine debris towards the centre of its loop. Researchers predicted the presence of such concentrated areas of floating debris in the 1980s and found the Pacific Patch in the same decade. In subsequent years, yacht crews elsewhere reported seeing plastic islands and soon other patches were found close to Japan and in the North Atlantic. Ocean scientists estimate the extent of the Pacific Patch to be 1.6 million square kilometres, although other estimates vary from 700,000 to 15 million square kilometres. The Patch is composed of around 1.8 trillion individual pieces of rubbish, and the waste objects range in size from discarded fishing nets to the tiny microbeads used in cosmetics and cleaning products. The estimated weight of the waste is 800,000 metric tons.

The waste that makes up these floating waste islands comes mostly from what we discard, and a large proportion (46% by some estimates) is from the fishing industry. But we landlubbers contribute too. Rubbish that's improperly disposed of ends up in rivers, storm drains, harbours and ultimately the sea. Even rubbish that is carefully put into bins can be caught up in the wind or carried away by animals or rain and washed out to sea. It's clear that here again, reducing our use of plastic will help reduce the problem, or at least stop it getting worse.

There are some innovative attempts to clean up these floating islands, silent witnesses to our love affair with plastic. A young Dutch inventor, Boyan Slat, imagined a simple but brilliant method for corralling and gathering the detritus bobbing in the Garbage Patches. A floating, anchored system of booms forming a rainbow-shaped giant scoop, several kilometres wide, would herd and concentrate plastic pieces so that they could be removed from the water. The scoop is propelled by wind, waves and current. Although the Ocean Clean Up project recently hit some teething problems, it still shows promise. One concern, reported in the UK press in January 2019, is that the floating barrier may crush species that live in the layer just beneath the surface of the sea, members of the 'neuston ecosystem'. These animals include jellyfish, sea slugs and snails. This top layer of the sea also provides a feeding ground for turtles and a nursery for fish. When currents and wind propel the barrier along and it scoops up jagged edged and rigid plastic waste, it will also take in soft-bodied animals such as the blue sea dragon. In the jumble of colliding waste, these animals risk being corralled, battered and suffocated.

The Ocean Clean Up boom recently fractured too and had to be sent for repair. There have been other problems: the winds pushing the plastic in the water at a speed the boom can't cope with, and plastic accumulating faster than the support ships can remove it. Another concern is that much of the plastic in the oceans is in tiny fragments well below the surface range of the scooping apparatus. The best solution still seems to be keeping plastic out of the sea by reducing our use of it. Scooping it out is likely to be complex and expensive at best.

Around the world, other initiatives are using different technologies to get some of the plastic out of the oceans. In Baltimore Harbour, the Trash Wheel funnels and lifts waste out of the water. The Great Bubble Barrier Project in Amsterdam uses a bubble screen to redirect floating plastic debris to the sides of rivers and canals while allowing shipping to pass freely. Elsewhere, Sea Bins, floating, pump-driven versions of the dustbins we use on dry land, are scooping up plastic in harbours and still-water areas. But these projects, while they offer a real, pragmatic hope for the future, are, if you can bear the terrible pun, a mere drop in the ocean when it comes to cleaning up the mind-blowing quantities of waste already in the water causing harm every day. When the quantifiers used are 'trillions' and 'billions', it's hard to picture what these levels of waste look like. Let's just agree it's a lot.

ALMOST ALL THE PLASTIC THAT HAS ENTERED THE OCEANS IS STILL THERE...

In 2017, a research collaboration between scientists at the University of Santa Barbara and the University of Georgia found that of the 9.1 billion tons of plastic manufactured since the 1950s, 7 billion tons are no longer in use. The researchers estimate that 9% has been recycled, 12% incinerated, and the remaining 5.5 billion tons have been discarded and now litter our land and oceans.

While recycling technology has advanced a lot in the last decade or two, the proportion of plastic waste that is put into recycling waste streams is dishearteningly low. The amount of material sent for recycling that can really be recycled is smaller still, for many reasons including contamination, wrongly classified waste, market-value fluctuations and logistical limitations (e.g. proximity and capacity of recycling plants, and problems with the scanning of plastics).

...BUT WAIT, THE WORLD IS WAKING UP

At the University of Tasmania, in 2017, researchers began looking at plastic waste on the sea floor, noticing that it had been largely neglected by studies to date and so left out of the already astounding statistics. If you thought the figures on plastic waste sounded big to start with, they're about to get bigger. Meanwhile, throughout 2017 and 2018 in the UK and many other parts of the world, news stories about plastic accumulating in rivers and on beaches began to impinge on the public conscience. Sir David Attenborough's *Blue Planet II* documentary series for BBC television, in particular, helped bring about this rapid sensitizing of public awareness to the problem. We may have reached a tipping point.

SO, WHAT'S TO BE DONE?

It seems the only workable answer to our plastic problem is to reduce the amount of plastic we use and find alternative materials and ways of doing things that don't rely so much on plastic, particularly single-use plastics and those not accepted into recycling streams via our home-refuse collections. While there is a UK government commitment within DEFRA's 25-year plan to stop plastic entering the ocean and other international accords, such timescales seem quite far off. If we produced nine billion tons of plastic in the 69 years since 1950, just think how much we might produce in the next 25 years with a population now on its way to eight billion.

Professor Richard Thompson, OBE, is a world authority on the problems caused by plastic pollution in the marine environment – and the potential solutions. Head of the International Marine Litter Research Unit at the University of

Plymouth, he coined the term, 'microplastics' in 2004 and discovered some of the effects of these tiny fragments on marine life at a time when other scientists were more concerned with plastic waste at the macro end of the scale. He was involved in work to change UK legislation on plastic bags and the ban on microbeads in cosmetics. As Professor Thompson told Jim Al-Khalili on BBC Radio 4 recently, it's not so much plastic materials that are the problem, but how we use them. He really believes we can turn around the plastic waste problem, but there's work to be done. The plastic packaging that confronts consumers in supermarkets, he says, is still far too varied and confusing. We shouldn't have to face an ethical dilemma over which packaging is best or worst each time we go shopping. The homework should be done for us so that we can be confident the products on offer are in packages with the minimum necessary environmental footprint.

Plastic drinks bottles are made from PET, an easily recyclable, high-value plastic, used successfully for years. Transparent PET bottles are widely recycled but when pigments are added or the bottles wrapped in sleeves made from other polymers, it complicates reprocessing and their value is reduced. If product packaging is designed from the outset with easy recycling and disposal in mind, we can move closer to a circular economy where waste is much decreased. When we reach a threshold where a much greater proportion of plastic packaging in shops is standardised – easily recyclable via simple-to-use disposal streams with clear markings, we the consumers will be able to confidently reduce plastic waste via recycling. In the meantime, we could do worse than follow Professor Thompson's lead in responsible plastics use: take a reusable bag when you go shopping and follow the common-sense '3 Rs' approach: Reduce, Reuse, Recycle.

GREAT IDEAS TO THE RESCUE

There are people working on clever ways to dispose of and digest plastics so that they don't pose such a threat to our environment. Still other clever scientists and product designers are working on substitute materials that look and behave like plastic but are in fact biodegradable, compostable films, such as David Christian's seaweed-based plastic-style film, Evoware, developed in Jakarta. Meanwhile, initiatives such as the Surfers Against Sewage Plastic-Free Community Accreditation Scheme add exciting incentives to join the fight against the plastic tide. In Indonesia, a Garbage Banks scheme offers payments to collect and bring in plastic waste to local sorting facilities and from there it is sold on to recycling companies. A Florida craft brewery working with a start-up company has developed a biodegradable six-pack ring for its beer, made from wheat and barley, that can be eaten by sea creatures rather than trapping them.

In Australia, a research team has hit the headlines by using tiny magnetic coils to dissolve microplastics and purge them from water. Although the process does create CO_2, the researchers are refining it and it holds great promise. In future, it might be possible to use this magnet technology around water outlets where microplastics enter rivers and oceans, removing the fibres before they come into contact with aquatic flora and fauna.

Other scientists are testing ingenious answers to our plastic pollution problem that take lateral thinking to a whole new level. One group is investigating certain moth larvae that are partial to feeding on PET plastic (used for drinks bottles). Another team is investigating plastic-digesting bacteria. The problems of raising enough of a population of these larvae and bacteria to consume plastic at scale are still to be worked through, but the ideas hold promise.

Inspired by an idea spotted in the Philippines, the Ecobricks movement has devised a way of putting unrecyclable plastic to good use by stuffing them inside plastic drinks bottles to make bricks for building projects. You can even make your own bricks, using the instructions on their website and take them along to one of their drop-off points.

Given that most gardeners are not based in laboratories or at the helm of companies developing breakthrough plastic alternatives, we must in the meantime find practical ways to work that don't cause further damage. The most effective thing we can do right now is to reduce our unconsidered use of plastic, especially single-use, non-recyclable forms and find alternatives that allow us to carry on with our hobby or work in ways we can sustain. This promises to bring benefits to the environment, today and in the future, and it may change the way we feel about our gardens. When we seek out other materials to fulfil the purposes for which we once relied on plastic, these options can often bring an enduring beauty to the garden.

ALTERNATIVES

This book will offer suggestions for avoiding plastic, reducing reliance on it (particularly single-use or disposable forms) and finding sustainable alternatives. That's not to say, and this discomfiting thought may already have struck you, that the suggested alternatives will be entirely without their environmental impacts and repercussions in other areas of concern. Metals like aluminium, for example, can cause environmental damage when extracted and processed, they require energy to smelt and forge and that energy in turn will likely use up fossil fuels and produce environmental by-products whether CO_2 gas, heat-energy waste or chemical discharges. Paper too, sometimes used for pots, has its environmental and labour costs – from extracting timber to transporting it, to the chemicals, energy and labour used to process it into the bleachy white product we scribble on and recycle for various garden and household uses.

Even recycled paper takes a lot of water and some chemicals to produce. Cotton – used to make the bags many of us now carry to substitute the ubiquitous plastic shopping bag – is not a product with a blemish-free ethical and environmental record. Some reports suggest that cotton in garments bought from many UK high-street retailers will have involved child labour in the chain of production. Cotton cultivation relies heavily on irrigation and the intensive use of chemical pesticides, herbicides and fertilizers. In some regions such as

Uzbekistan, cotton growing has been linked to desertification of large areas of once arable land. A cotton tote bag has to be used 149 times before it can be deemed to be carbon neutral, i.e. have offset the carbon footprint of its production and supply. This is according to one report on how UK supermarket 'bags for life' are not being used enough (eight times at least) to offset their carbon cost.

According to the designer Philippe Starck, plastic can often be the best material for many functions. When you take a broad view of the alternatives, often touted, without much justification, as 'natural' and 'eco-friendly', the environmental and social costs of their cultivation, extraction and processing can be far worse in some cases that those of a plastic item. "(Is there a material that you could immediately reject?) Yes, all the natural materials! Wood. Wood has to stay in the trees. Leather has to stay on the cow. Everything that kills any vegetable or animal should not be used! Or, until we have an alternative. Today, it is completely archaic to destroy forests or to kill animals. It is a regression of humanity. And it is a stupid strategy." ('Material Tendencies', *Architonic*, www. architonic.com, 23 June 2015.) A radical view perhaps, but in the search for a way through our plastics quandary, occasional doses of lateral thinking and unusual perspectives can be illuminating. When an alternative to plastic is offered, there is no simple strategy for weighing up its full costs and impact against that of the plastic version. It's always going to be complicated, but this book will attempt to offer some ideas and general guidelines. Ultimately, as Starck says, the best policy may be to simply take a more moderate and thoughtful approach to consumption, "to make less – less design, less material, less energy … to end up with more."

In each case, the suggestions offered here will try to give a balanced sense of the benefits of switching to an alternative material or technique, leaving readers to make their own judgement after weighing up the options. The development of alternatives is moving swiftly and the market changes almost weekly, so regular reviews and updates will be needed to be sure you're finding the best products for your needs. And beware, the path to plastic-free gardening will not be smooth and edged with roses and lavender all the way. Alternative products are not well developed or tested in many cases, and the labelling and terminology is dishearteningly, confusingly and outrageously inconsistent, misused and abused. You will find products labelled 'Eco', 'green' and 'biodegradable' that you consider to be anything but. And beware words like 'natural', 'environment-friendly', 'plant-based' and 'degradable' (everything is degradable if you wait a few millennia).

There will be some frustratingly incongruent little surprises along the way, like plastic-free products arriving virtually mummified in many layers of … plastic! Plastic tags, bags, rigid packaging, tape and price stickers will continue to appear on your plastic-free products. When this happens, it's a chance to let the supplier know that it bothers you and why, but it seems certain that change away from plastic for all these elements, from packaging to labelling to secure pricing and tracking systems, will take time.

The pace of change may also be accelerated by legislative developments. The UK government published a Resources and Waste Strategy (December 2018) which will consult on a tax for packaging products with less than 30% recycled content and on a deposit return scheme for single-use plastics, as well as implementing measures that will make producers fully responsible for disposal or recycling of packaging waste they create. The strategy also aims to streamline recycling schemes, so they are more consistent across all local authorities. These changes will affect the horticulture trade and should reduce plastic waste over time. Governments in many other countries are consulting on or trialling similar proposals.

What would be a proportionate response to our plastic problem? Some commentators express concern that the plastic issue is stealing all the limelight, to the detriment of other environmental threats of equal or greater importance and urgency. That may be the case, but it is very likely that the huge public interest in reducing plastic use will lead to increased interest in, and motivation to tackle, other environmental problems too. When people 'do their bit' to clean plastic off a beach or take fabric shopping bags to the supermarket, they tend to feel motivated to do more for other related causes. We can hopefully harness the attention being given to plastic waste and turn it into a positive change that eventually becomes the norm, rather than a fad that sucks our attention and energy away from other causes.

The problems with plastic can seem overwhelming, but lots of people the world over are feeling that way and it's giving them the motivation to make changes. While scientists and engineers develop clever new materials and ways of working, there's a lot that gardeners can do by making small changes, following the reduce, reuse, recycle approach and sharing their ideas with others. The information in the chapters ahead will focus on substitutes for many of the materials and objects we use in our gardens, as well as different methods or approaches to doing things that can reduce the need for plastic. In each case, there will be personal factors to consider like cost, convenience, durability and compatibility with your existing methods, lifestyle and tastes. I will try to give options that are reasonably priced and not too labour intensive; they have to be otherwise the chances of them being adopted by a significant number of gardeners, enough to make a difference, will be slim. As policy makers and economists know very well, the incentives and nudges influencing our behaviour and purchasing habits must be structured just right in order to bring about the kind of tipping point that leads to large-scale change in consumer behaviour and choices, the kind of change we need to reduce the negative impact of plastic on our world.

Avoid	Try
Think twice before buying new plastic products, especially single-use and non-recyclable plastics.	Seek out alternative materials: paper, metals, wood or vegetable-based alternatives to plastic. Read on.
Buying products labelled 'Eco', 'green' and 'degradable' that don't offer transparent information about these claims.	Opting for products labelled 'compostable', 'home compostable' and ideally those that disclose their ingredients – e.g. 'corn starch'.
Discarding plastic materials that can be reused, unless you can deposit them into a recycling scheme.	Look after and reuse garden equipment and supplies, plastic or otherwise.

2

PLANT POTS

When you think of gardening and plastic, what are the first things that come to mind? With me, and with many gardeners, it's pots. Square or round, nine centimetre or five litre, terracotta coloured or (overwhelmingly) black, the little containers we use to sprout our seedlings or carry our new plants home from the garden centre all have one thing in common: they're made from plastic. Even more concerning, they are apparently non-recyclable (or *are* they? More on this later…) which compounds the sense of guilt and wastefulness. But, since it often seems we have little choice but to buy more plastic pots if we want to have plants for our plot, or containers for our bulbs, seeds and cuttings, many gardeners just suck up the guilt or turn a blind eye. Apart from a rueful shake of the head when tossing them into the general waste 'landfill' bin later on, or a vague pledge to reuse them (yes, along with the many hundreds stashed in the shed) we try not to think about our contribution to the plastic waste problem.

Plastic plant pots are often made from different plastics to those used in food packaging and this is given as one reason why so many local authorities are reluctant to take them into kerbside recycling schemes. In some regions another reason is given: soil contamination. Even when pots are made of the same, common plastics as found in food packaging, there seems to be a problem with their black colour – a result of the carbon-pigment they contain. Black plastic doesn't reflect enough light, making it hard for the light-based sensor on the sorting equipment in recycling warehouses to read the symbols indicating plastic type. It can be hard for the human eye to read recycling symbols on black plastic, even on food packaging. Add to that the mix of different plastics that have been used in the past to make pots, and confusing or absent markings on some pots to indicate to consumers whether they can be recycled, and it begins to be clear why they're seen as mostly non-recyclable. Most new black plastic pots are made from recycled post-consumer and industrial waste materials – e.g. from car manufacturing. This extruded polypropylene is a good quality plastic that has high value for reprocessing. But the potential to continue the recycling loop after gardeners have used them is frustrated by the confusion over symbols, acceptability in domestic waste bins and the problem with sensors at sorting facilities.

The statistics for the industry as a whole are sobering: one estimate suggests there are 500 million pots 'in circulation' in the UK each year (*Which* magazine, 2011) – presumably this means on garden centre or nursery shelves or being taken home by customers at any one time. It doesn't take account of the stacks from previous years many of us already have lurking in the back of the shed. Some pioneering garden centre groups have been trying to change this situation by offering recycling schemes that collect customers' used pots and make new membrane, sheeting or plant pots from them. But these have been relatively small-scale, local operations with limited coordination. Schemes like this also rely on finding a specialist plastics reprocessing company near enough not to incur significant transport costs, and a willingness to dedicate staff time to receiving, sorting and packaging returned pots. It also depends on customers remembering and making the effort to return their pots; only a small percentage will manage this. On top of all these factors, the market value of plastics changes, so what works as a recycling loop one year may not be viable the next as the materials might not be worth enough to justify transport and processing costs.

A small garden centre sells around 40,000 potted plants per year. They rely on wholesale nurseries to provide their stock and have to accept whatever pots it comes in. But there are good reasons why the black plastic pot has become ubiquitous. They are economic, durable, light and cost-effective to transport, as well as being stackable and hygienic. They fit together neatly in trays (mostly) and on shelves and protect plants very well in transit. They also promote root health by absorbing warmth through their walls yet keeping light away from photosensitive roots and letting excess water drain out, directing it down their gently sloping sides through the small holes in the bottom.

Garden centres have no use for old trays and can't return them to suppliers for fear of spreading pests and diseases. Pot manufacturers also tweak the size and shape of their design now and then, leaving growers (domestic and industrial) with pots that won't stack together. It's a similar situation at supermarkets and DIY chains who also sell plants. In view of all this, tackling the plastic pot status quo looks like a mammoth task.

The National Trust vowed in 2018 to move to biodegradable pots at all its properties within four years. This and similar moves by other larger national plant sellers signifies an important change. The customer feedback antennae of these organisations have been twitching as visitors make their feelings about plastic known. The fact that large bodies with hundreds of outlets and properties that include thousands of acres of gardens have made the pledge to move away from plastic sets an example. This will undoubtedly send ripple effects through the market and reflects a changing public mood.

WHAT TO DO WITH YOUR POT STASH?

First, to address the little (or huge) stack of plastic pots you already have. Those you no longer need, or which are damaged can be taken to your local recycling site and added to the plastics recycling bay. This way there is a better chance they can be recycled than if they were put into kerbside bins. It's not every council recycling facility that has a plastics recycling bay, however, as I discovered recently. Pots surplus to requirements at the Trellis Potting Shed must be put in the Non-Recyclable Waste skip as the council currently offers no way to recycle them. There is clearly work to be done to make local authority recycling programmes more comprehensive and standardised. It's worth asking your council if you can put plant pots into the kerbside plastics collecting bins and remember this may change over time. If you find your area doesn't offer pot recycling through any channels, perhaps your local garden centre might operate a pot return/recycling scheme. There is a UK-wide scheme backed by the HTA (Horticulture Trades Association) for member garden centres to join, with plastic reprocessing by Hampshire-based Ecogen Recycling. In practice, however, it works out prohibitively costly for garden centres north of Birmingham to take part, though new schemes are under development. Failing that, if you have family or friends in a neighbouring local authority area that does offer plastic recycling, perhaps they can take them for you.

For those pots you can still use, look after them. Exposure to sunlight can make them brittle and prone to cracking so store them in a dark shed when not in use. Likewise, clear pots (e.g. for orchids) and clear plastic lids for individual pots or larger propagators can become cloudy with exposure to sunlight, so keep them in the dark too when not in use. Taking care of the plastic pots you do have will hopefully prolong their useful life so that you can reuse them many times before taking them for recycling. Meanwhile, when buying new pots or plants, try to opt for non-plastic ones, or those that clearly state they are recycled and recyclable, where you can.

BIODEGRADABLE POTS

In 2010, an article in *Horticulture Week* magazine reported that all the major pot suppliers were now offering biodegradable ranges. This sounds like great news for ordinary gardeners seeking alternatives to the conventional pot materials. But progress towards seeing these widely supplanting the ubiquitous black plastic pot has been slow, partly because of concerns over cost, but also because of worries about how their biodegradable counterparts might perform in the production and handling stages of horticulture supply chains.

Biodegradable plant pots are made from quite an array of materials including corn, coir, wood chips, rice husks, potatoes, miscanthus or seaweed, often bound together using plant-based solidifying agents such as latex and starches. These materials are trialled and developed over time as producers refine their product to reduce problems of robustness, biodegradability and appearance. Some of the less rigid models, in particular coir pots, can be planted out into the garden directly in their pots and the plant will root through the pot walls.

Jiffy Pots

Jiffy, a Norwegian company, offers peat-based biodegradable pots and has sold these for years – but many gardeners don't want to use peat as a raw material because of concerns about its sustainability. And that is just one example of how complex arguments about environmental issues can be. The Jiffy peat pots have been refined so that nurseries can now print their logos on the sides and they're fully compostable after use.

Coir Pots

Most famously used by the Hairy Pot Company for the plants they sell, coir (coconut fibre) pots can be used for bringing on plants (they'll start to look quite hairy after a season of watering and sun) and planting out. Once planted into the ground, plant roots can easily find their way through the pot walls into the surrounding soil to seek out water and nutrients. Meanwhile, the pot fibres themselves will slowly break down and become part of the soil. Various online suppliers sell coir pots including The Green Gardener.

Cow Pots

Based in the US, this company makes pots from cow manure. A great way to divert and make something of value from a true 'waste' product. Not widely available in the UK and probably not likely to find favour with some vegan gardeners.

Plant Starch Pots (various)

Trials in Germany at The State Teaching and Research Institute for Horticulture (LVG) in Heidelberg tested eight brands of biodegradable pots and compared them with their plastic equivalents. They raised crops of Petunia, Nemesia and Mandevilla and found in many cases the performance of the biodegradable pots was as good as that of the plastic ones. The trial found "near-identical plant quality" for the petunias and good performance with the other crops too. Fungal growth and cracking were noted in some of the pots, but the harder pots (those made from potato or corn starch) needed very high temperatures to be broken down, and these conditions are really only found in industrial composting. This is a problem with many products labelled 'compostable'.

A French company is making pots from potato peels with thinner base sections to enable more effective composting in the ground after planting. A Dutch company is making pots from potato starch and says they will only biodegrade after being in the ground for three to four years. Pots that can be put into domestic composting would be a great development. However, this will have to be balanced with the need for durability in pots.

Perhaps in future we'll be offered choices in garden centres that ask us to choose between pots for long-term planting displays and more temporary homes for seedlings, propagation use and transplants. Indeed, this may be a useful way to approach your pot purchases in general. Although it won't always be possible to find the right variety of plastic-free pot you want (especially when you're seeking out a particular plant specimen, rather than purchasing empty pots for raising your own plants at home), as the market develops, the range of options should improve. If you're buying pots for short-term use – for seedlings or softwood cuttings, say – that will be potted on within the season, you could opt for compostable pots. When buying pots for more permanent plantings, more enduring materials such as terracotta and metals would be better.

Swiss company Napac sells NaturePots made from rice or reed fibre, glued together with plant-derived binding agents. These performed well in the German trial. In the UK, NaturePots are distributed by Soparco who also sell their own organic divided modular pots and trays made of wood fibre.

Vipots are made from rice husks held together and made rigid with plant-derived binding agents. We've been trialling these at the Trellis Potting Shed. They seem sturdy and apparently last four to five years but will biodegrade within 18 months if broken up and put into compost. This is the manufacturer's claim and we have not tested the compostability of Vipots.

Posi Pots

Foldable card pots (used by the Edible Culture Nursery in Faversham) that can be used for transporting, displaying and planting out young plants without needing to remove them from their pot. They are quite thin card so wouldn't be a lasting option but will readily rot down when planted out.

Bamboo Pots

Bamboo pots look as sleek and rigid as plastic, it's hard to believe they are biodegradable. Hard, durable and not prone to swelling or warping in humidity or extremes of temperatures, these are worth a look. They don't however come in a range of practical shapes and sizes to replace all your current growing needs, not yet at least. Also, the paint finishes and coatings used may involve polymer resins so you may need to give bamboo-pot brands closer inspection before being sure they will be a good plastic-free choice.

Paper Pulp Pots and Trays

These are recyclable, can be composted or will breakdown relatively quickly in landfill. Several generic options are offered online and in garden centres with varying levels of detail disclosed about provenance and manufacturing processes.

The horticulture packaging firm, Modiform, offer a range of 'EcoExpert' trays made from the pulp of recycled paper.

POTS OF OPTIONS – RESULT CONFUSION?

Cost still seems to be a major factor limiting the mass production and availability of alternatives to plastic pots: it costs suppliers more to make these pots and they pass on some of the cost to customers. This means that retail customers have to be willing to pay a little more for their non-plastic pots.

And it may also mean garden centres may stock fewer of them: the extra cost may put off all but the most environmentally dedicated (or better off) customers. This may also mean that while biodegradable pots remain a niche product, it's likely that the particular plant(s) you want to buy will be in plastic pots, so there will still be no option but to bring home more plastic if you want new plants.

Some manufacturers and suppliers of plastic containers have launched new products from plastics that are recyclable, for instance carbon-pigment free polypropylene pots (i.e. usually not black), suitable in theory for kerbside recycling collections. However, there still lots of barriers to recycling many plastics, not least the fickle forces of the market demand and the attitudes of different 'gatekeepers' at the various stages of the recycling chain. The reason many councils won't accept plastic pots in kerbside collections is not solely because sensors can't read recycling symbols on traditional black pots (and so can't sort them from other waste). They also have concerns about collecting pots in quantities that will have enough market value to make the costs of sorting and transporting them viable.

The huge variation between the recycling rules and systems of different local authorities only adds to the confusion. Across the land, people who want to recycle pots are not sure if they will be accepted by council collections, while others remain convinced pots must not be put in the recycling bin, even though, after a change in policy, their local collection does now take them. In addition, there's at least a lingering idea that pots must be cleaned before recycling, whatever the local rules, and this might seem a step too far for people with busy lives and priorities other than washing up for the recycling collection.

Some incentive programmes have been suggested – for instance, deposit return schemes or a tax on plastic pots, similar to the five pence on plastic bags that so revolutionised our shopping habits. These might be worth looking into but require coordinated effort across many sectors and legislation too which can take time. Voluntary efforts may have the potential to effect change more nimbly, as they rely on simple agreements between businesses and trade organisations that are already motivated to respond to customer demand.

With all the widespread confusion about plant pots, many people, perhaps the majority, assume they're non-recyclable (when technically, even the black ones are, if only the infra-red sensors on the sorting machines could recognise them as such). Because of this, hundreds of thousands of pots will still be thrown into landfill because people don't know what else to do. In addition, there's the well-known blight on refuse systems the world over that a lot of material that can be recycled is not simply because it's not put into the right bin or indeed any bin, but disposed of in some other way, so never reaches the recycling plant. As we've seen, many campaigners for plastic reduction would urge us not to use 'biodegradable' or 'degradable' plastics as they can create problems including extra emissions. Such materials may also use up a lot of energy and greenhouse-gas-increasing chemical additives to produce.

You might wonder whether making changes in your own garden can ever have an impact if industry and authorities are still going to use plastic at substantial scale and make recycling tricky. The environmental footprint and purchasing might of such organisations dwarf the puny cries for change of individual gardeners. Arguably, unless big nursery growers, pot suppliers and the huge plastics recycling firms change, the home gardener can't achieve much: it can feel pretty deflating. Happily, there are changes coming. The packaging industry is already forging ahead with new products and the horticulture industry has moved with incredible speed and breadth, to increase plastic recycling and switch to products that can be reprocessed easily. The next challenge is in improving the information offered to consumers and changing the perception of plastic pots so that people know what they're buying and how to recycle it. This is going to be achieved partly by changing the colour of the traditionally black pots.

IS TAUPE THE NEW BLACK?

With impressive dynamism and efficiency, garden centres across the UK have adopted taupe-coloured pots in response to customer concern about plastic recycling. As part of a huge and extremely far-reaching scheme pioneered by the Horticultural Trades Association (HTA, the UK industry body) and its members, taupe, a light beige colour (for those of us not au fait with the interior decorator's lexicon) was chosen to differentiate pots from the old-style black ones so that people know they can potentially be recycled in kerbside collection schemes. These taupe pots must be made from 95–98% recycled plastic and be fully recyclable. Taupe and other colours of pots are now available in garden centres across the UK. Around the same time as the taupe revolution, one company developed a pigment that would allow traditional black pots to be detected by recycling plant sensors. But so swift and complete has been the mass adoption of the new taupe as industry standard that no one wants a black pot anymore. Although it's inspiring to see how quickly change can happen, some teething problems are anticipated with this colour revolution.

One area of concern is standardisation of size and markings, which affects how well they might fit in recycling bags and bins, how easily they stack for storing and how well the markings will guide disposal in the correct waste stream. Some schemes in Germany and other countries have introduced pots of standard dimensions – something that should also reduce problems with storage and transport. Size standards aside, the taupe pots may simply still not be accepted by a huge proportion of local authority kerbside collection schemes because many councils fear they won't have enough volume to make separate collection and processing viable. It's simply not always cost effective for them to make big changes to their recycling processes. The huge variability between the UK's local authority schemes further complicates the taupe pots story. This is being highlighted by nursery and garden centre owners and also on the BBC *Gardeners' World* programme in summer 2019.

More consultation and collaboration are needed. The HTA and its members are already on the case, talking to local authority environment teams directly, with promising results. One nursery representative who was closely involved in developing HTA policy on plastic pots has been meeting people from the three local authorities closest to his business. When council managers saw the taupe pots and understood their recycling potential, their attitude to accepting them in kerbside bins improved. One commented that soil residue on pots would be far less of a health hazard than the food waste refuse crews encounter on plastic packaging that is accepted in household bins. We gardeners can help augment this change by talking to local councillors to make them aware of the improvements in the design and manufacture of plant pots that make them easier to recycle. Meanwhile, attempts by the horticulture trade to persuade the big plastic repro-cessing companies of the market potential for recycling plant pots might just be starting to change perceptions.

The plastics recycling business is a little like a food chain. At the top are the big companies that can process plastics and make them ready for moulding into a new product. If they won't or can't give a decent price to the people who collect plastics and bring them for recycling, such as local councils, it creates a huge deterrent to collecting plastics at the next link down the chain. If local councils fear they can't sell used plastic to the big operators at a reasonable cost, they're unlikely to want to collect these materials. The councils set the rules for what householders can put in domestic refuse collections, so if they say no to plant pots, the home gardener has little option other than perhaps to take pots to a local garden centre if there's one with a recycling scheme. To some extent, government also exerts influence near the top of the chain. They may impose legal limits on councils, insisting that they meet certain recycling targets. But they also influence the operations of the big reprocessing firms. If plastic manufacturing, moulding and reprocessing companies work together with the horticulture trade and local councils, they can create a circular system where reuse and recycling is designed in from the start.

credit: Stan Green, Growforth Ltd

The UK industry is very aware of the importance of environmental concerns to its customers and of the scale of plastic packaging waste associated with the purchases made in pursuit of the nation's beloved gardening hobby. Surveys by *Gardeners' World*, government and for trade bodies show that UK consumers are concerned about waste and its impact on the environment, and feel commerce is not doing enough to reduce packaging waste. Gardeners tend to show a greater than average concern for environmental issues, at least in surveys, and many feel far too much plastic is used in gardening, with pots seen as the biggest problem. The taupe pots may go some way to making people feel a little better about the plastic associated with their gardening. This still may not be good enough, however, for many who hope to see plastic vastly reduced if not completely removed from the production chain, and urgently.

The owner of the Hairy Pot company has been using coir pots for many years now and he has seen demand for plants raised in coir pots skyrocket. This accords with the findings of the HTA, which has noticed demand for non-plastic pots rising among garden centre customers, especially in 2018. When the industry recognises these signals from its customer base you can be sure that change is not far off. And that means we may be slowly but surely getting closer to a threshold where non-recyclable and unrecycled plastic pots could soon be a thing of the past.

This could be a problem for the many sellers and manufacturers of plastic pots and packaging that supply the horticulture industry, with jobs and businesses at risk. But just as all industries have to be smart and adapt to changing market demands, the pot trade is already working on new technologies. We can expect to see all kinds of products in the near future, pots and trays made of cardboard that's been treated to prevent sogginess, and 'plantable pots' made from tomato stems – stable above ground, but quick to decompose in contact with soil. Another design that's compostable after drenching in hot water is also ready for market.

As with all seismic industry changes, customer demand combined with technological and supply-chain capacity will hit a point beyond which the only sensible way ahead will be to adopt alternative products and offer them across the market as the new norm. With big wholesale customers like the National Trust and Natural England switching away from plastic pots, it's a good sign that large-scale change is not far off.

Be an active consumer: let your local garden centre and nursery know that you want to buy compostable pots and help the change come faster. Try to buy from nurseries that use non-plastic pots, or at the least use recycled, truly recyclable pots, and support those that run a recycling scheme.

Alternative Pots to Buy or DIY

While the industry gets to grips with testing and marketing its compostable pots, there are lots of options for the home grower to use in the meantime. There are pots made from well-established alternative materials that you can buy and reuse and some you can make for yourself.

BUY, BORROW OR INHERIT

Most people have too many plastic pots, so if you're starting to garden for the first time or need more pots than you have for a special project, you can probably find them by asking for donations from the gardeners you know.

Terracotta and Ceramic Pots

The traditional model has perhaps yet to be bettered. Clay extraction and mining for glaze constituents all incur emissions whether in the form of fuel to power the modelling and firing processes or as by-products and run off, but the humble and ancient terracotta pot is hard to beat. Terracotta is porous, so it lets excess water seep out, whereas ceramic pots, being glazed, are not, except perhaps at the base. Efficient as conductors of heat, clay pots warm the plant roots and potting medium inside them, and they're easy on the eye, perhaps the reason why the design has barely changed in centuries. Stackable, sturdy and easy to handle, they can be scrubbed up for reusing year after year. For some, scrubbing clay pots would be heresy, as the weathered look of terracotta is highly prized. Used as a permanent planter, exposed to the elements and micro fauna and flora in your garden, clay pots will, over time, develop an attractive patina of mineral and oxidation deposits from hard water, leaching of fertilizer elements and air weathering effects on the clay, algae, moulds and sun discolouration. This ageing effect only adds to their charm. In fact, it's so popular that many people paint plastic pots to look like aged terracotta, or paint yogurt onto virgin clay pots to attract microorganisms.

Clay pots are heavy of course and that's not something to be dismissed lightly for many of us, especially if you have back problems, arthritis or other health conditions that make carrying clay pots (especially when full of wet soil) difficult. Suggestions for reducing the weight of pots include using lightweight drainage 'crocks' to line the bottom of the pot, such as scrunched-up thick paper instead of stones or fragments of other pots. Also, mixing light-as-air Perlite or Vermiculite into the compost mix will help make the whole pot lighter. Consider setting clay pots on wheeled bases.

Terracotta pots can dry out a little too fast, but there's not much wrong with them other than that. With proper firing and good quality clay, the traditional garden pot will withstand extreme cold, and can be insulated with hessian if there's a worry about cracking or plant roots freezing in the depths of winter. Given that 'frost proof' labelling terms are inconsistent and possibly not well controlled, the chances of buying a pot that does not withstand severe winters in one piece is moderately high. Add the risk of shattering or chipping pots in the normal course of handling them and lugging them around the plot, and there's a good chance you'll end up with a collection of broken pots. Many gardeners simply collect these casualties to use as 'drainage crocks' in the bottom of other containers.

There are also some manufacturers making pots that are more reliably frost resistant, such as Yorkshire Flowerpots. As a rule, I don't expect pots made in warm, tropical climates where the temperature almost never drops to zero to be sturdy enough to stand up to the cold of a UK winter.

Orchid fans: don't worry that you need those special translucent plastic pots to let the light into your plants' roots. Special terracotta orchid pots are available with large holes cut into the sides, designed to let orchid roots run free.

Wooden Pots and Trays

Whether your preferred seed sowing method is to fill trays with compost and sow into that or sow into pots then stack those into trays, it's a fairly safe bet that alongside the towers of plastic pots in your shed, there may be a fair few plastic trays too. Instead of using plastic trays for your seed sowing, you could consider returning to wooden trays, which were the standard before plastic took over and are currently enjoying a resurgence. You can find them on sale in garden centres, from companies such as Nutscene and via various online shops including vintage ones from resellers such as Ebay.

Those with some basic carpentry skills and a little time could also have a go at making their own from scrap wood such as pallet wood. Drainage is via gaps between the slats on the bottom of the tray, or you can drill holes if the design does not include gaps in the base. Typical dimensions are approximately 39 cm by 25 cm by 6.5 cm (depending on how you plan to use the trays). Some people use wine or brandy crates begged from wine merchants, although these are harder to find now as their value and supply chains are changing.

Wooden trough or box-style planters and even small wooden containers for individual houseplants can be attractive. Sometimes they're lined with a zinc inner pot or the interior painted with varnish to make them last longer. Wood pots generally benefit from a little maintenance painting to extend their life by protecting them from the elements. While plastic pots and trays are easy to clean, wooden models can rot and harbour pathogens as they age, so clean and dry them after use and store in a dry place to prolong their useful service.

Cardboard or Pressed Paper Pots

As noted in the list of biodegradable pots, these are available cheaply from several suppliers, made from recycled paper pulped and compressed into pot shapes. A great alternative to plastic for seedlings and small plants, these are a temporary growing vessel as the paper won't last for more than a few months once wet and in contact with soil. But as plant roots grow through the walls of the softened paper pot and begin to be air pruned, this way of raising young plants can create a healthy root system. It avoids pot binding where roots grow round and round the inside of a pot, creating a rigid tangle that won't anchor the plant into the soil and let it establish so successfully as one that is planted out before becoming pot bound. Planting seedlings into the ground without having to remove them from their pot is less labour intensive and avoids transplant shock, a state where plants are set back in growth and may wilt and look poorly for a few days as they recover from damage caused to young roots by pulling them out of their pot. There can be some problems with paper pots losing their shape, tearing and attracting mould growth. Suggestions for dealing with these are set out later in this chapter.

Cellulose or Paper Bags, Pots or Tubes

Some seedlings for agroforestry projects are now being raised and transplanted in cellulose bags and tubes. Made by Danish company Ellegard, bags, pots and tubes fashioned from banana fibre and cellulose from other plant sources are being used by many different growers across the world. Compared with polythene bags in trials, these paper-based bags seemed to allow plants to root faster, maintain optimum levels of soil humidity (because they drain better, allowing water and air to pass through) and they may even produce a harvest in a shorter time. The pots biodegrade in soil, which means plantlets don't need to be taken out of their seedling pot to grow them on, so reducing or avoiding transplant shock, which can set plants back. These mechanically produced cellulose pots and tubes are more resistant than the home-made newspaper or cardboard pots domestic gardeners might use and have a more sophisticated design including perforations to allow air pruning and healthy root development. For now, this seems to be a product aimed at commercial growers. But if consumer and legislative pressures encourage nurseries and growers in the UK to offer more alternatives to plastic pots, we might have a chance of seeing them in retail outlets soon – both the pots themselves and plants for sale that have been propagated in cellulose pots.

The Paperpot System

The Paperpot System is aimed at market gardeners growing at some scale and is not entirely plastic-free. But its ingenious paper cells might inspire new ways of working for home gardeners. The system is based on a honeycomb of paper cells which are delivered flat-packed like Christmas decorations, then opened out, concertina style, set in a plastic tray (long lasting, recyclable), filled with soil and sown, one seed per cell. Once the plantlets have developed, they can be planted out in record time using a narrow metal transplanting cart that feeds the cells into furrows, one row at a time.

Zinc and Other Metal Pots

Metal pots can be attractive and practical for certain growing situations. They are ideal for established decorative plants, especially house plants. It's best not to use metal containers for seedlings and young tender plants since the conductivity of metals mean they transmit extremes of heat and cold, stressing the plant roots which can lead to weakened or even dead plants. For situations such as roof and balcony gardens where weight is a consideration, metal pots can be a good option, being far lighter, in general, than terracotta. These situations, however, tend to be even more exposed to extremes of sun and high winds. Lining metal pots inside with fabric or even cardboard might be wise, to help avoid any scorching or over-fast drying out of the compost and roots.

LOOK, NO POT!

Soil Blocking Tools

These metal contraptions are the old-school way to raise seeds and their design has stood the test of time. Blocking tools use no pot; instead, they depend on compressing compost with the correct consistency and water content into rectangular blocks that retain their shape until the seeds sprout and take root. The blocks need to be set into a tray, ideally a wooden seed tray. Thereafter, the root networks of the young plants maintain the shape of the potting blocks and are air pruned as they reach the edges of the compost. The trays of compost blocks make a good alternative to modular trays.

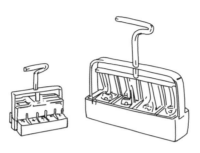

Soil blocking tools are essentially metal forms with several chambers and a spring-loaded handle to squeeze compost out in rectangular modules. The blocks need to be firm enough to hold their shape until the seeds germinate and grow on to the potting on or planting out stage, because there is no solid external membrane (such as a plastic pot) to contain the soil.

The trick is in getting the compost mix to the right consistency and this means combining the ingredients of your compost recipe correctly and, crucially, adding just the right amount of water – which is probably more than you think is sensible. The mix may seem awfully wet, but this is the secret to getting the blocking tool to mould your compost into neat, stable shapes with divots pressed in their centres, ready to receive a seed. Soil blocking offers a rare thing – a simple, tried and tested, low-cost method of forming growing media into an efficient shape for raising seedlings, with minimum material wastage. The spring mechanism forces some of the liquid out of the wet compost mix, so that when you carefully push the blocks out of the bottom and draw the frame off the top you're left with lines or grids of four, eight or 16 blocks (depending on the size of your blocker) ready for sowing. While many recipes for the best compost mix for soil blocking insist on peat, others say that a mix of loam or topsoil with peat free compost and vermiculite does the job.

Using a soil blocker can take a little practice but should pay back your investment over time in money saved on pots and will certainly reduce the amount of plastic used to raise plants.

Pellets or Jiffy Pods

These compressed discs of coir (and sometimes peat) can be expanded in water to form small oval-shaped blocks of growing media ready to take a seed. They can be very useful but beware – many of them come in a plastic mesh wrapper. Reject these and try to find pods that are plastic-free and fully compostable. Coir extraction in tropical regions of the world may have some environmental impacts, including some salt water run-off, as detailed under the discussion of carbon foot-prints, but on the whole, it doesn't seem to have seriously harmful effects.

REPURPOSING

Toilet Roll

Simply piled into a box or biscuit tin and filled with compost/soil/your growing medium of choice, these cardboard tubes are a quick and easy way of using up waste destined for the recycling bin with no extra effort required other than remembering to save them. They make a good alternative to Root Trainers, those long plastic pots moulded into rows of four that open by folding apart like a book.

The elongated shape of cardboard inner tubes from tissue rolls is ideal for legumes like peas, beans and sweet peas as they love a long, deep root run. You can plant the tubes straight into the garden as the roots will sprout through the wet cardboard. Some schools and other groups have decided to ban using toilet roll inners in this way over hygiene concerns. This may be an overreaction considering there are probably more harmful germs on the average smartphone or laptop, but perhaps chopping kitchen roll inners in half would be a good workaround. Cardboard is subject to some of the same disadvantages, mentioned later in this chapter, as DIY newspaper pots – fungal growth, erratic drying out and so on, but you can adopt simple measures to minimise these problems.

Some people like to use a four-way folding technique to fashion the end of the kitchen or toilet roll tube into a flat, enclosed base. This can create a nice solid bottom, allowing each 'pot' to stand alone and reducing the likelihood that compost will fall out, but it also reduces the length of the tube.

Egg boxes can be used for raising seedlings too, although they are a little shallow so the young plants will need potting on quickly.

Heating Ducts, Drainage Pipes and Teapots

We've all seen them, charming or not so charming examples of crockery, sanitary ware or building materials dragooned into garden duty. From the wildly cute Instagram or Pinterest page full of Japanese *mame* cherry trees in diminutive teacups to inspirational gardens punctuated by beautiful zinc water tanks reborn as desirable planters, there's no denying repurposed domestic and construction items can make for beautiful garden displays. The usual candidates include everyday items such as bricks (plant Sedum and Sempervivum in the holes), old chimney pots (used as elevated planters/features, great planted with grasses or trailing species) and discarded washing-machine drums or sinks.

Many people delight in repurposing oddments of unwanted or leftover construction materials and domestic articles for garden use. Shiny heating or extraction ducting is a favourite as it comes in cut sections that lend themselves to different sizes and heights of planting. The different finishes of metal components, from gleaming steel to mottled zinc or muted copper, can work well as a design feature, depending on your garden style.

DIY POTS AND RECEPTACLES

Before the plastic age, we still managed to grow plants – we just used other methods and materials. We can revive some of these approaches and explore new ideas to reduce plastic use today. Here are some options to consider.

Paper Pots

As outlined in the previous section, paper pots are available commercially but there are plenty of options for making your own too. You can make pots for free using old newspapers or any household paper, perhaps misprinted pages from your printer, though any wastepaper should work. It's quick, very easy and strangely satisfying. You can use a bespoke pot maker which is usually carved from oak or some other hardwood.

These are available from horticulture retailers and gift shops both on the high street and online. Wooden pot makers are beautiful things in their own right: hand- or machine-turned wood, with two parts that fit snugly together and a smooth, ergonomically pleasing design that makes the process intuitive and stress-free. They are very long lasting since dense, resistant woods are used. Wooden pot makers usually come with instructions but essentially involve wrapping paper around the top, cylindrical piece leaving a margin of paper overlapping the end of the wood. Then, the end of the resulting tube shape is squashed into the bottom section of the wooden mould to make a closed, firm base.

If you don't have a pot maker, you can use a glass or bottle (ideally not a plastic bottle, but realists will recognise that until we reach a single-use plastic-free nirvana, many of us may have some of these lurking around at home). A small juice glass is about the right size. Fold a sheet of newspaper in half along its length (you could also use brown parcel paper) and wrap around the bottom half to a third of the bottle or glass to form a tube shape. Then fold over or squash the bottom down on a table or flat surface so that it stays closed to contain the compost you're going to fill it with later. You may also want to tape, clip or staple the side and bottom of the pot to keep its shape more securely.

Paper pots are usually best packed together in multiples of six, eight or ten inside a larger container or box so that they prop each other up. The most obvious containers to use in the past may have been plastic seed trays or old plastic fruit punnets. But since we're trying to find alternatives, you might use a wooden seed box or some other non-plastic container such as a sweet tin or catering sized peach or tomato tin that will hold several paper pots together and keep them upright.

Tin Can Plant Pots

Empty tin cans can make handy pots for growing on seedlings and young plants. The top rim where the can opener has left the edge a little jagged should be sanded smooth. The bottom should be punctured, perhaps with a tin opener, or a nail or bradawl, to make some drainage holes. Apart from that, you can use the tins as soon as you've finished the contents for dinner, and they don't cost you extra since they're a by-product of your weekly shop.

Recycling your baked bean tins as plant pots might seem more than a little homespun, but I was surprised to learn that this is in fact how container growing was done in the UK in the 1950s. Nurseries collected used tins discarded from households, punctured the bases and planted into them. They were treated as a single season item as rust would start to set in, but this practice continued until the mid-1970s. We can take heart from the fact that professional growers used this method for growing on plants in not so distant times.

It goes without saying that preparing used tins takes more time than just picking up purpose-made plastic pots. Tin cans will rust and rot over time too, when exposed to rain and irrigation. However, they can be charming and attractive for a year or two and they're a good size for growing on small plants. If you don't mind the extra work, it's a worthwhile way of spending a little free time.

Some people like to turn tin can plant pots into a whole craft project: they can be painted, and very keen craft-lovers also like to make patterns on the sides of tins using nail holes which can create an attractive effect. This kind of perforation pattern can also transform tin cans into lanterns, which, with the addition of a wire handle and a small candle stub or tealight, can be hung around the garden. The glow of candle-light through the punched hole patterns creates an interesting and delicate effect.

Recycled Vegetable or Fruit Skins

Planting into vegetables or other organic materials is not for everyone, but you can sow seed into eggshells, avocado or melon skins and the peels of halved grapefruit. These materials may not provide ideal drainage conditions or shapes for raising seedlings but may be worth experimenting with since they're waste products and biodegradable. It may be a fun project rather than your go to, long-term replacement for plastic pots.

Kokedama

The Japanese art of raising bulbs or other plants in a soil ball that is then bound with moss and twine and can be suspended from a tree or indoors, from a hook. The moss binding is designed to be as attractive as the plant itself. You can find instruction videos, images and diagrams online as well as a fabulous Trellis factsheet on our website.

credit: Joan Wilson, Trellis.

Reusing Food Cartons

Another option is to reuse plastic from food products, such as yogurt pots or drink cups as pots. One experienced gardener advises me that juice cartons with the top side cut off make good seed trays. This of course is not entirely getting away from the use of plastic in your garden. But given it is currently tricky to avoid plastic in your weekly food shop altogether and will be for a little while yet, reusing plastic items you've already bought can be a useful stop-gap solution. The good thing is that this kind of plastic waste, unlike plant pots, can go directly into the council recycling bins, so long as you rinse off any traces of soil.

PROS AND CONS OF HOME-MADE PAPER AND BIODEGRADABLE POTS

Drying Out/Sogginess

It can be harder to manage the humidity of the growing media inside your paper or corn-starch pots. Terracotta pots are also prone to becoming quite hot and allowing the soil inside to dry out, but gardeners have worked with them successfully for centuries. In most cases, it's just a case of monitoring irrigation and adapting accordingly to suit the needs of your plants. Just as the advice for houseplants is to water only when the soil feels dry when you poke a finger into the top layer, so plants in your garden or greenhouse should be watered only as needed. Waterlogging or dehydration are common problems affecting plant health at all stages of development and if we have become used to working with plastic pots, adopting a new system will need a period of observation and adjustment.

Fungal Growth and General Sliminess

Biodegradable pots of many different types, especially the paper or cellulose based kinds, have been found to develop moulds and even mushrooms on their surface in a way that plastic pots don't. The first thing to say is that most of these fungi don't generally seem to be a problem for the health of the plants, apart from, possibly, very young seedlings. General plant hygiene principles apply: you should encourage air circulation by spacing seeds out so seedlings are not too crowded and by using vents in propagator covers and greenhouses to ensure fresh air is getting in and around your young plants. Another tip is to start with good quality sterile seed compost that will have fewer mould spores in it from the outset of your sowing endeavours.

A less commonly heard idea picked up from blogger, The Unconventional Gardener, is to use a little diluted chamomile tea when watering seedlings as it has antifungal properties. It can treat existing mould growth as well as acting as a preventative. This is backed up by a citation by James Wong in his book, *Growing for Flavour*. There's the often-overlooked practice of observation and keeping ahead of the march of the moulds; pot on your affected seedlings into fresh clean compost and pots or into their permanent planting position at the first sign of fungus.

Disintegration and Resilience

Paper and cardboard pots can quickly become very soft and prone to sagging, falling over or tearing if you need to weed them or move them. This malleable property can be helpful as it lets you squash more pots into a tray. But it means each pot really needs other pots to keep it upright, so sowing into a single pot is not terribly effective for anything more than a very short-term arrangement. It's not uncommon for the bottom to fall out of a pot when you go to pick it up and unless you're ready to plant it out or pot it on right then, that can be inconvenient. But there are industry-standard pots that are designed to expose plant roots to the air to promote 'air pruning' (when roots grow out of a growing medium and are exposed to air, that encourages other roots to branch and stimulates stronger, more vigorous root growth all round) so having roots exposed is not necessarily a disaster. In custom-made air pruning pots, however, root tips reach the air gradually, so suddenly having long stretches of roots open to the air may be a shock to the plant.

To get around this, it's best to use paper pots as a temporary vessel for bringing on seedlings or small plants. Try to pack them snugly into a crate so they help keep each other upright. Plan ahead to minimise the need to move them. Ideally, once you put them into a box, all full of compost and seeds and set them out ready for watering, they will only be moved again when it's time to transplant them.

Size

The other limiting aspect of paper pots is that this perishable tendency means they're mostly only good for planting seeds or holding small transplants and seedlings. They really are not useful for older and larger plants since they're just not robust when scaled up and become a little mushy after a few rounds of irrigation. Hardwood cuttings, for instance, that need to stay in their pots for months to root, would not work in paper pots. The simplest way to circumvent this would be to propagate these cuttings in a trench in the open ground.

New cardboard pots are in development that contain an inhibitor to prevent them getting soggy. Even with an inhibitor, cardboard looks likely to remain a material used mainly for small to medium sized pots.

Unsightliness

Soggy newspaper or toilet roll inner pots can look a little sad and unsavoury, especially when they've developed a thriving culture of fungal colonies on their surfaces. One solution is to modify your watering so that plants are not constantly damp, so limiting fungal growth. Potting on when pots start to look too bad is also good practice from a plant hygiene perspective. Trying different brands of paper-based pots may lead you to one that is less prone to losing its shape and attracting moulds. Switch to wooden seed trays or soil blocks and skip pots entirely if you just don't fancy having soggy paper pots in your garden. On the positive side, soggy, partially mouldy paper is a perfect carbon-rich addition to the compost heap to help balance out nitrogen-rich green materials.

Time (and Effort)

Clearly, it's much quicker to grab some plastic pots that are ready made than to have to make a batch of pots before even starting to sow into them. Although if you factor in the time taken to travel to buy the plastic pots, perhaps you could make paper pots in the same time, or less. Given we are all more likely to describe ourselves as time-poor today, despite evidence that we have more leisure time than in previous decades, making plant pots can seem a step too far. Many of us may feel it's already hard enough to make time to sow some seed or spend half an hour weeding the garden. If other commitments force you to prioritise your garden tasks to fit a short time-window, perhaps buying pre-formed pots made from paper pulp or coir would be the way to go.

Traceability

We don't know enough about some of the products being marketed as biodegradable and plastic-free. Often, it's a new or experimental product and so regulations and supply-chain documentation can be slow to catch up. This means it can be tricky and time-consuming to make a like-for-like, fair comparison of products to decide what is really the best choice if you want to reduce plastic use.

Plastic in the Mix

Many biodegradable pots may not be as plastic-free as you think. Some use synthetic binders which often contain plastic. Look for a 'fully biodegradable', or better still a 'compostable' label. Many paper pulp pots seem to mix peat into the product description, and the product itself, which complicates things a little for many who want to avoid using peat. The market is full of unbranded pots with meagre information about the materials that have gone into their production, so a bit of reading around or questioning is needed to be sure of what you're buying.

Carbon Footprint

Plant pots made from corn and other biodegradable materials are not necessarily carbon-free, carbon neutral or even less carbon-producing than their plastic equivalents. They still involve extraction of raw materials while the processing and energy required to turn the ingredients into a pot will likely be responsible for emissions and waste products too. And then there are social questions and secondary environmental impacts to consider.

In Sri Lanka where many coir pots are produced, the coir is

dried in the sun so there's not a huge amount of additional energy required for this phase of processing. Coir is shredded coconut husk fibre. While the husk is generally a waste product, extracting it from the hull and shredding is a mechanised process powered by quite a bit of energy. The coconut husks are soaked, often in sea water, for a long time to help the extraction process, and there can be some run-off, potentially into local water sources, when they are rinsed. The pots are made by hand, so it provides jobs for local people. But in the case of other pots made from the husks of rice grains, or from miscanthus (tall plants of the grass family) and other materials, our understanding of the industrial process and the traceability of the production chain and its social impacts is less than comprehensive. This will hopefully improve with time.

Paper, of course, also requires lots of energy and water for processing wood pulp or paper and may also use bleaches. Fossil fuel generated energy and the effects of possible water pollution must be factored into the equation when deciding between paper pots and plastic or other choices.

In addition, many materials labelled 'compostable' in truth require industrial composting treatments that use heat and are very different from our own home composters. Commercial composting facilities may not always be available close to home. There's also a lot of confusion about how to dispose of such items to ensure they go into a waste stream destined for industrial composting. Should we put 'biodegradable' bags and plant pots into the council garden waste bin and assume that it's all heading for the necessary heavy-duty industrial composting? Or will that contravene local authority refuse collection rules? There is no clear guidance in most regions of the UK, and householders are often left in confusion as to how to dispose of such items.

Another problem is that materials that look like plastic but are labelled 'biodegradable' may release additional methane and other greenhouse gases when decomposing and may have had a biodegradation accelerant added during manufacture which is often a substance with a negative environmental impact. These products are not therefore a simple or clear improvement on plastic pots that may be recyclable (if the collection and reprocessing loop is easy to access) and typically are also made from recycled materials.

In the quest to diminish plastic waste in our gardens, it's not always easy to know if the alternative methods or materials of choice are better overall, or if there might be pernicious downsides.

A helpful idea is to seek out dependable sources of information, e.g. websites that provide up-to-date information on new products and their environmental impact. These sites should be neutral if possible, i.e. not profiting from sales of a given product, and using transparent methods, clearly explained, for their evaluations and reports. Ethical Consumer is one website that some people like, although it has relatively little gardening content and gives higher scores to organic and non-GM brands, having made assumptions that these production methods are best, which not every expert would agree with, from every perspective. By reading up on the criteria and rationale behind their judgements, you'll get a sense of whether these sites' reports are what you need. The Business and Human Rights Resource Centre provides analysis and briefings on whether businesses around the world respect human rights and includes an environmental section.

Investigative and consumer journalists and campaign groups

will occasionally investigate products that are reaching a certain market threshold, and these reports may be our best way of understanding the full costs of a given product or material. As the market changes and the scale of production increases, labour conditions will also be in a state of flux. This means ethical assessments of how each product reaches our shopping basket and ultimately our gardens will also change, possibly quite rapidly as manufacturing develops to keep up with demand. Transparency and traceability will vary and so the work of monitoring the production chain of these alternative products will likely be tricky for a while yet. Hopefully soon, some of the non-plastic pots will emerge as superior to others and claim their place at the forefront of the market, making it easier to track production and enforce the relevant regulations.

Avoid	Try
Pots claiming to be 'biodegradable' or 'compostable' with no further information offered.	Coir pots or pots made from bamboo, rice husks or plant starches.
Pots made from black or coloured plastic with no clear recycling information on them.	Terracotta pots, the original and best. Making your own pots from paper or kitchen-roll inners.
Polystyrene plant and seed trays.	Soil blocking tools. Wooden seed trays. Tin can pots or repurposed crockery or building materials.

3

TOOLS AND EQUIPMENT

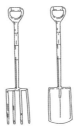

Many gardeners have a special affection for old, time-served things; articles that are handed down and treasured from another age or found and reused. They particularly love glass and wood, things forged from iron or steel, preferring materials not too far removed from their natural state over plastics. After all, working among natural things is what gardening is all about, right? A generalisation perhaps, but that was how I liked to see things – that is until I took a long, steely look inside my tool shed. Indeed, there were lots of things that were very, very old and had been inherited or bought second hand, possibly third or fourth hand, and stood the test of time because they were solid and well made.

My turf cutter, for instance, has a beautiful angled neck leading to a long wooden shaft and a deep, D-shaped handle carved with an unknown gardener's initials. If you're anything like me, there will be many other such ancient tools in your shed, things of great beauty, the handles carved with the initials of long ago owners, reminding you of your place in a line of gardeners whose hands and years of labour polished the wood and burnished the metal. Sitting alongside all the old and beautiful things, however, are plenty of things made of plastic. They slip into the tool shed, into your shopping basket without you really noticing. You go out in search of a lightweight trowel and it turns out that the only model on offer that's any lighter than the wood and metal ones is plastic. The same Hobson's choice situation arises when you're in the market for a lighter watering can. I really shouldn't make excuses for the many plastic items in my shed; suffice to say the report card summary reads, 'Could do better'.

Spades, Forks and Rakes

These tools are mostly made from wood (often ash) and metal, perhaps carbon steel, although sometimes coated with Epoxy resin – that's right, a plastic. When the basic model is adapted for comfort or convenience or to reduce its weight, that's often when plastics are added. Some tools will have foam trim added to the handle to make it soft and more comfortable. There are spades with a circular handle designed to allow them to be gripped from different angles. The handle is made from plastic.

Chillington Tools is an interesting company to explore, selling 'traditional tools' with a wide range. The handy thing is you can buy handles and tool heads separately, so if you want to replace the head of a favourite spade or rake, but keep the very comfortable handle, they can help. They also sell extra-long wooden handles which are often a great investment as many tools are sold with a too-short handle: a sure-fire way to end a day in the garden with a very sore back.

Finnish company Fiskars make a lightweight range of tools, called the 'Light' range in white or black painted aluminium with steel. They are very nice to use and don't seem to involve much or any plastic in their construction. Some of their other tool ranges, however, do have plastic and fibreglass in their handles.

Spear and Jackson also offer spades, forks and rakes with stainless steel heads on hardwood handles. But they sell tools with plastic handles too, which seems to be true of many of the main tool suppliers. Online shopping does let you explore the construction materials used in different tool ranges before you buy. Nothing beats going to the garden centre though, to heft a spade in your hands and see first-hand what it's made of.

One other idea is to investigate tool libraries in your area. The option of being able to borrow the tool you need from a central collection organised by a group in your community would certainly help reduce the plastic you use. Not every town has a tool library and you may need to use most tools more frequently than practicable for a communal borrowing programme, but it could be an interesting option for scythes, say, or lesser-used tools.

Small Hand Tools

In this category you are likely to find tools made wholly or partially from plastic, especially when seeking lightweight models. There's not really any reason to buy a dibber made of plastic, when the turned-wood, metal or bamboo models are easy to find, cheap, and possibly lighter. But for customers searching for a light, cheap hand fork or trowel, often plastic models seem to fit the bill best. I have it on good authority from a gardener with arthritis in her hands that with small hand tools, excepting badly designed, very heavy tools, the weight is not so much of a consideration when balanced against cutting power and design. If a tool is well shaped, sharp and efficient, that often matters more than how lightweight it is. Indeed, plastic trowels and forks are often too rounded and blunt to be effective, which can cancel out any advantages claimed for their lightweight construction.

The good news is that there is quite a range of decent plastic-free options at reasonable prices. Most of the main tool manufacturers produce high quality, lightweight hand tools made of metal and wood. Other good sources of hand tools (as well as spades, rakes and so on) are the increasingly common community tools refurbishing projects that offer restored, second-hand tools (for gardening and increasingly also for carpentry and other crafts). In Edinburgh, Garvald is one example (most of their restored tools are shipped to communities in developing countries, but the surplus is sold off at their Christmas Fair), but some other charities and community projects offer this service, and indeed certain prisons have become involved too.

IRRIGATION

Watering Cans

Old-style zinc or enamelled watering cans are good options, although plastic models are often much lighter. It's a good idea to have more than one size of watering can so you're not having to lift or carry more water than necessary. Keep watering cans around the garden at the places you'll need them most, to further reduce how far you're having to carry them. Another more passive way to tackle watering is to use an immersion vessel of some sort: a shallow, water-filled tray or bowl for sitting pots or seedling boxes in. Old sinks or baths are sometimes used for this, and you could also use an old roasting tin. Once your pots have soaked up the water they need, lift them out and set them down wherever you want them to grow on.

Hoses

Some hoses are made of rubber or latex/silicone mixes, others are plastic: vinyl or PVC. Hoses are likely to last a while, five to ten years if you protect them from the worst extremes of weather and try not to trample them or run the wheelbarrow over them too often. With this in mind, the hose may be an example of a product where buying a plastic version perhaps would not be such a terrible thing. However, latex hoses are widely available, affordable and are often the best quality options on the market, with good resistance to weather and sometimes wire mesh inner layers making them even better able to cope with variations in temperature and the abuses we gardeners subject them to. Vinyl or PVC hoses are often lighter and cheaper but are more prone to cracking, kinking and degrading if left out in the elements. From this perspective, there are probably few reasons to recommend a plastic hose over a latex one.

However, rubber hoses can be heavier so in some circumstances this may be a more important consideration than the ultimate environmental impact. Hoses made from a rubber-vinyl mix are also available and may be a useful compromise for weight/cost and resilience. Note that both plastic and rubber (latex) hoses can leach chemicals into the water so don't drink from them and buy a pet-safe hose (polyurethane) if your pets will drink from them.

When it comes to connecting your hose to the tap or to other hoses and nozzles, brass fixings often make the most durable and watertight options and are affordable and widely available. Plastic connectors frequently fracture and develop annoying high-pressure leaks that soak the gardener more than the plants, so there are additional reasons to opt for brass.

Drip Irrigation Systems

These systems tend to comprise either networks of narrow black plastic ducting that can be hooked up to the areas and plants on which you want to focus irrigation, or 'leaky hose' or 'leaky pipe' systems. These are rubber hoses with lots of little perforations to let the water out, designed to be laid a little way under the soil surface near plant roots. The narrow, above ground systems seem to be made of plastic throughout; however they are extremely efficient, being targeted and steady, and use significantly less water than other systems. The leaky hose systems are more interesting from a plastic avoidance perspective and are generally effective, bringing water straight to the roots where plants need it most. These porous hoses are often made from recycled car rubber. They're also a good choice for water conservation as there is no waste from water being dripped onto the leaves or the soil surface, only to be lost to evaporation.

Water Butts

A water butt can be a great resource-saving device, albeit most commonly made of plastic. Alternatives are wooden barrels or terracotta models, undoubtedly more expensive, or perhaps a discarded tank from a heating system or a trough from reclamation or agricultural salvage yards. These will often be made from zinc or aluminium, though they are not widely available as second-hand items. In some houses, if a new boiler has been fitted, there may be a disused water tank left in the loft. Bringing this out via the typically small loft hatch can be a challenge but if it's possible the tank may make a perfect water butt.

The guttering and downpipe that lead to your water butt are also likely to be plastic as are the connectors. It is possible to get metal downpipes and guttering, but they are generally expensive too. The answer may be to live with the plastic pipes and try to spend money on the water butt itself to avoid buying new plastic there.

Water butts are likely to last for ten years or more and can be recycled along with other rigid plastics, so may be one of the more acceptable plastic items in your garden.

Spray Bottles and Misters

For keeping certain tropical plants and small seedlings watered, especially indoors, a fine spray of water is ideal. While we've become accustomed to using plastic spray bottles, their predecessor, the brass misting spray, is every bit as good and far longer lasting. The added bonus is that they are handsome objects in themselves, which is more than we can say of the plastic variety. Happily, there seem to be several companies producing brass or brass and glass plant misters, perhaps thanks to the revival in popularity of house plants, so they're easy to find.

CUTTING, PRUNING, CARRYING AND STORING

Scythes and Grass Hooks

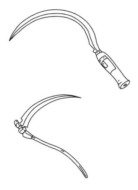

Once a common sight in rural Britain, the scythe has become a romantic artefact that only a few dedicated souls know how to wield. But it is an alternative to the plastic strimmer thread we so often turn to for long, rough grass and wildflower meadows at the end of the season. There is an art to using them – it takes practice, perhaps a little tutoring. The bonus to a little time spent learning how to use a scythe is that you will reap benefits to physical fitness. Monty Don prefers Austrian scythes as they're lighter, apparently, than UK ones.

Grass hooks, the scythe's smaller sibling, are not used very much more commonly but are very handy for trimming long grass in small corners. They look very much like the sickle from the Communist Party flag, symbol of the peasantry appropriately enough for gardeners. I have never seen a grass hook with any plastic components and think this may be one tool to purchase safe in the knowledge it will be plastic free.

Secateurs and Loppers

The range of secateurs on offer in UK garden centres now is happily very good and includes a lot of very nicely made forged steel models with wooden handles. Of course, there are many models also on offer with handles containing at least some plastic, but these are avoidable.

For gardeners who have a lot of pruning work to do each year, the handles of their secateurs need to be soft and not cause blisters and rubbing. This need for a more forgiving and comfortable grip is one of the reasons that manufacturers add plastic to the handles of their tools. It might be possible to bind wooden handles with some soft fabric to make them gentler on your hands. Some people will wear gloves, especially since a lot of pruning work is done in the colder months. But other gardeners feel that their grip is compromised by gloves. For many, the ergonomic properties of hand tools like secateurs are paramount and it would seem more important to buy the comfortable secateurs in order to keep gardening (and so benefit your health), rather than make life difficult and unpleasant just for the sake of avoiding bringing home a small amount of plastic. Secateurs are hardly a single-use item (although the clumsier and more forgetful among us may not keep track of them for as long as we might like).

Well-made secateurs with wooden handles can be supremely comfortable, especially once they're broken in after a bit of use. I've used secateurs with plastic handles that caused terrible blisters. The material is only one part of the puzzle, so don't assume wooden-handled tools won't be best for comfort.

Loppers, likewise, will be made mostly from metal, but will typically have plastic handle covers to improve grip and comfort. This is a safety feature as much as for ease of use and it's hard to see a way around this for now. Once again, well cared for loppers will last – perhaps for a lifetime – and so won't be heading for landfill any time soon.

Knives

Opinel make great knives, well-suited to gardening and allotment life. They are foldable and have handles made from different woods including olive and cherry. Treated well and regularly sharpened (some models are more complicated to sharpen, so consider this before buying) they will cut through twine, bags of soil, marrow stalks and can even whittle wood, as well as slicing cucumber for your sandwiches. There are lots of cheap knives on sale with plastic handles, but many affordable alternatives so you needn't be stuck for choice.

One gardener I spoke to in researching this book swears by the *kirpi*, or Indian hoe, a hand tool that she reckons can replace most garden hand tools. Best described as a cross between a small grass hook, a billhook and a knife. It's said many people won't go back to using a hand fork after weeding with a *kirpi*. The tools are often of rustic construction, made by Indian blacksmiths and have a serrated section as well as varying angles to the blade that really help the gardener get at weeds, whichever awkward position they may be growing in.

Waste Disposal and Carrying

The buckets and trugs we use for transport and storage are inevitably made from our old friend, plastic. Trugs and builder's buckets are as common on the average plot as slugs and worms. They're so handy, for lugging around compost and transporting weeds, stones or whatever you're tidying up to the compost bin or the turf pile. But what to use instead if you're trying to reduce your reliance on plastic? For harvesting and carrying small or more delicate items, there's the classic Sussex Trug, typically made of split sweet chestnut or willow, and a thing of great beauty. Several businesses are still making trugs in the traditional way in Sussex and now offer online sales. You might take a look at Thomas Smith Royal Sussex Trugs and Charlie Groves' The Trug Store.

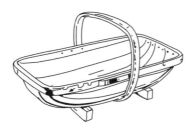

For more substantial loads, you can buy wooden buckets from companies that make barrels, but chances are they are heavier than the plastic buckets we're used to. Many are marketed as 'medieval' or 'decorative' and you may well agree that those are good descriptions after trying to use them as functional replacements for the lightweight buckets we know well in the 21st century.

Enamelled tin or zinc buckets are widely available, partly thanks to a revival in vintage-style homewares. You can find them sold as 'ash buckets' but also as storage bins for household cleaning equipment. They're probably not going to be so light, convenient and comfortable to handle as the sturdy plastic bucket we're used to, but perhaps that's just a prompt to reconsider how we work in the garden and find a different approach. For instance, if you're collecting weeds in a bucket with the idea that once it's full, you'll take it over to empty into the council waste bin: perhaps instead, wheel the council bin over to where you're working and put the weeds directly in. Or use a wheelbarrow.

Another option is to spread a waxed cotton canvas tarpaulin over the ground to catch weeds, prunings or loose soil while you work. With some rope threaded through the eyelets around the edge, tarpaulins can be gathered up into a sack or envelope shape for easy transportation. They can be hosed down and hung up to dry if they get muddy and periodically reproofed with proprietary waterproofing products. Dan Pearson talks about using one in his book, *Home Ground: Sanctuary in the City*. The tarpaulin is just visible in one of the photographs: he's using it to contain compost and spills while potting plants. Muddy Faces and Tarpaflex both sell waxed cotton canvas tarpaulins in the UK.

Baskets, woven from rattan, willow, reeds, split wood or seagrass on a frame, are another option for carrying things –

larger weeds, produce and hand tools. The willow basket, like the Sussex trug, is another great traditional UK craft product that has stood the test of time and is still in production today. Baskets designed for garden use (such as flat, shallow styles for gathering cut flowers) are available at very reasonable prices, made by local craftspeople from British-grown willow. Try Coates Willow for starters, or Somerset Willow. Willow baskets last for years if well-kept and can be brushed out to clean any soil residue. Like all useful things, they will repay the care and maintenance you give them with longer service. Wire baskets can also work – line with a cloth or newspaper if gathering fine weeds.

Wheelbarrows

Many are still made with a galvanised metal pan, although there are lots of barrows with a plastic body now for sale, often marketed as being lighter than the metal models. Whatever the main material used, most wheelbarrows come with plastic handle covers too. If well-cared for, a metal wheelbarrow can last for many years. There are lightweight aluminium styles on offer that may offer a happy compromise between the desire for levity and rustproofing and the wish to avoid plastic. Storing a barrow under cover will help extend its life.

Tool Stores

Now you've got your plastic-free tools, where are you going to store them? Traditional timber garden sheds are another of those designs that have stood the test of time. But there are several plastic tool stores on the market as well as tool hanging racks, stands, 'organisers', shelves and other tool shed 'accessories' made wholly or mainly from plastic.

There's not a huge amount to say in favour of plastic tool stores over timber models, from a plastic reduction point of view. Of course, a plastic store requires little or no maintenance but arguably won't last nearly as long as a timber shed. I've seen many a vintage shed with claims to wartime antiquity. Many timber sheds are not painted all that often and yet stand the test of time. Plastic, on the other hand, is likely to degrade with a few years' exposure to UV light, rain and algae. Plastic tool stores don't really need any building beyond minimal assembly and can just be plonked in situ and put to work – another appealing convenience. But if the walls warp in extremes of weather, they can be hard to put back in place so that the door shuts snugly. With a wooden shed, you can always realign the timber with a few nails and a hammer. Finally, plastic tool stores have often been seen as the most space-saving option for a small plot. Timber sheds are now available in very slimline proportions, however, to fit in the tiniest nook of the narrowest garden. Even the shallowest timber shed offers Tardis-like storage as the walls can be sawn very thin, whereas plastic shed walls are typically quite bulky.

If you inherit a plastic tool store, it makes sense to use it, but there are not many arguments for buying a new one.

When it comes to kitting out your shed and storing your tools efficiently, there's plenty of scope for avoiding the plastic racks and stands on the market. One of the simplest tool hanging methods is to knock pairs of nails into a beam or cross strut with just enough space between them for a tool handle to fit comfortably. Leave the nails sticking out at least 5cm proud of the wooden strut. Stow forks, rakes, trowels or spades by sliding the wooden handle between the nails until the head of the spade, or the D-shaped handle rests on top of them. Being too wide to pass between the nails, the tool head or handle stops it sliding down. The D-shaped handle of spades and forks can also be hung over the two spaced nails, a little like hanging a coat on a hook.

With timber sheds, there's lots of wall space as well as vertical and horizontal struts on which to install wooden shelves and whichever metal and wood hooks and hangers you need to store your gardening equipment. In a plastic store, you have to rely on custom-moulded storage hooks and plinths, as the walls don't lend themselves to affixing shelves or racks with nails or screws.

SUNDRIES

Ties and Twine

Cut up old towels, sheets or tee shirts to make ties for securing your plants to their trellises and wires. Or use old-fashioned twine, bought wrapped in paper not plastic, or indeed unwrapped, or in a tin for easy dispensing. Twine can be suspended from a piece of bamboo with a wire hanger threaded through to let it spool out.

You can also make your own dispenser for string or twine using a jar with a hole punched in the lid through which the twine can be pulled without knotting or tangling. As ever, it's sensible to sand smooth the rough edges around the perforation in order to avoid cut fingers or frayed twine when using such a home-made dispenser. Lots of twine is also sold in custom-made dispensing tins with a hole in the lid for running the twine through. Nutscene is a great supplier of twines made in the traditional way using the same original equipment since 1922. Their twines come in a rainbow of shades and they have lots of other alternatives to plastic on offer (dibbers etc). See the supplier listings at the end of the book.

Garden centres, craft suppliers and even gift shops have a veritable cornucopia of natural fibre twines, cords and string to offer us from seagrass to raffia to sisal, nettle and hemp yarn. There are garden twines on the market made from waste wool and others made from cotton, linen and reeds. Some people may have seagrass left over from a furniture making or repair project or raffia for floral arrangements that they could reuse for tying in plants in the garden. With all these alternatives on offer, this is probably one of the easier areas in which to avoid using plastic in your garden.

Labels

The ubiquitous white plant labels we know so well are made from plastic. While some diligent souls remove the wording each year with sandpaper, a pencil eraser or white spirit, the labels do grow brittle with exposure to sunlight and soon snap after a season or two. Given this tendency, they can almost be classed with single-use plastics, since after one season helpfully displaying the name of the first crop they are planted with, they often snap, sometimes into many pieces, reaching the end of their useful lifespan. In some cases, they last long enough to display a second year's or late season crop name on the reverse, but if they're exposed to enough sun over a full summer season – marking long-season crops like broccoli, for example – they will be rather fragile after only one outing.

Small fragments of plastic can be harder to recycle than more sizeable items, and of course, even if we did want to put labels into the recycling bin, most labels do not offer enough surface area on which to display the symbols that direct them to the correct recycling stream. Being dotted with compost, and very obviously non-food waste, they will also not be welcome in most council kerbside recycling bins. The need to find an alternative is clear.

Hopefully plastic plant labels will be swept up by the same reforming broom that's changing the plant pot industry and new, ingenious designs will soon hit the market. Meanwhile there are already a few alternatives to consider, both retail and home-made.

- **Slate** – either bought or home-made, slate makes a handsome material for plant labels. Broken roofing tiles may have naturally divided themselves into handy label-sized pieces or can be cut (wear goggles!). Some slate labels are hung around tree and shrub branches, by means of drilled holes threaded onto a loop of wire like a necklace, while others are stuck in the ground in the same way as conventional white plastic labels. Names and planting dates can be written on with a traditional slate pencil although this can be a little faint. Alternatively, you can use paint, a white wax china pencil or pale ink marker pens and possibly even chalk, depending on how exposed to the elements your label will be. Nutscene is one supplier of slate labels (see the supplier listings at the end of the book). If you know a friendly local roofer, you may be able to negotiate an endless supply of broken roof tiles for use both as a landscaping material and as labels.

- **Wood and bamboo** – wood labels large and small are on offer in gift shops, farm shops and garden centres, in all varieties of painted, waxed or unadorned wood. If you buy unwaxed wood labels, it's a good idea to paint them before use as such thin wood (often softwoods) will rot quickly without protection. But you can also recycle lolly sticks, fashion your own labels from offcuts of wood or use bamboo, old clothes pegs, dowelling offcuts, driftwood and even wine bottle corks. Thin softwood labels, even when painted, will disintegrate sooner than thicker labels made from oak or other hardwoods which should last a few seasons.

- **Tin, copper, aluminium** – these are traditional materials for labels in the horticulture trade and can be bought in various shapes and designs: as tags to be tied around plant stems or trunks with wire or stake-in-the-ground style labels with pointed stems. With copper labels, often a sharp nail or a bradawl is used to write or emboss the name of the plant into the metal. You can also use printer's embossing letter sets which are hammered lightly into metal to create an impression and spell out the variety name, letter by letter. Aluminium and tin may also have names scratched or imprinted into their surface or you can write on the metal with marker pens or paint.

- **Steel** – some manufacturers offer laser-printed steel labels. More expensive than plastic or wood, they could be seen as an investment for labelling specimens that you expect to be in your garden for the long haul.

- **Waxed card** – some nurseries use waxed card labels to identify varieties on trays of plants. The waxy covering makes the card waterproof for a limited time – this type of labelling is also used in the catering trade. It can be a short-term solution for plant sales and displays but won't work as a lasting system for more permanent planting. On the plus side, card labels are readily biodegradable and compostable.

- **Sea-washed glass, seashells, pebbles or brick pieces** – collected on holiday or from your local beach, or even dug up in your garden – can make attractive labels. Glass that has been tumbled on the waves until its edges are worn smooth takes on an opaque, frosted quality that makes it easy to write on and read and an attractive way to mark a bed or a plant.

- **Broken or discarded crockery** – as with glass, only safe, smooth-edged fragments can be used, though sharp edges can perhaps be ground or sanded smooth or covered with glue / resin, thick paint or some other substance to make them safe (though glues or paints may introduce some plastics to these plastic-free labels). If you search online and in some garden crafts books for images, you'll find some pretty examples of old plates and teacups used as plant labels. You can write on them with marker pens or china wax pencils. It's a whimsical option, but a way of using up unwanted pieces, and of course, avoiding plastic.

- **Textiles** – taking inspiration perhaps from wishing trees or 'clootie trees' in Scotland, Ireland and other parts of Northern Europe, ribbons or strips of fabric are sometimes tied to plants to identify them or inscribe some other message or information. While the ink will run and fabrics may fade and fray in time and look a little mildewed or even be nibbled by insects, they can make a beautiful, ephemeral way to label plants or parts of the garden, whether with botanical details or some other story linked to the particular specimen or location. To increase longevity, waxed fabric could be used.

- **Air-Dry Clay/Modelling Clay** – for the craft-minded gardener, making labels from a clay that doesn't need firing might be an appealing option. You can buy air-dry clay from craft supply shops and online, but do check what each product is made from – some such as the famous Fimo brand, are made from a PVC polymer, essentially a plastic, which we must assume will pose the same problems as the plastic labels we're trying to replace. Other air-dry clays are closer to the traditional earth clay that goes into crockery and plant pots. Or there are recipes online involving cornflour for making your own clay at home that the truly committed DIY and craft fan might enjoy, though beware the ones that involve white PVA glue, also a polymer. There are lots of instructive websites and online videos offering tutorials on how to make plant labels from this kind of clay and some beguiling ideas for imprinting plant names and decorative touches. I haven't found any testimony about how long they might last if stuck in the wet soil of a potato bed during a typical Scottish winter, but perhaps readers might share their experience of using these labels in such testing conditions for future editions of this book. We encourage readers to share their ideas via the #plasticfreegardening hashtag.

- **Terracotta** – terracotta labels are sold by some suppliers, but they tend to come with a limited range of plant names imprinted in the clay, usually the common culinary herbs. However, some blank terracotta and ceramic labels are available, for instance from handmade tile companies like Aldershaw. Often, they are sold in small quantities as a gift rather than a functional item for home growers of any scale, so they may be relatively expensive. But if switching away from single-use plastics is as much about a change of mindset as of our purchasing habits, it may serve as a good prompt for us to consider whether we really do need labels in the packs of 50 or 100 we'd typically buy when plastic labels were the go-to option. Perhaps, if labels are going to be with us for ten years or more, investing in a few longer lasting ones will seem like economic good sense and we can change our habits to suit.

Many gardeners, and I include myself in this statement, buy too many plants and sow too many seeds. If we follow the Reduce-Reuse-Recycle mantra, this tendency would be reined in. We would sow fewer varieties, a tried and tested clutch of favourites with perhaps one or two novelties on trial each season, and fewer individual seeds, just enough to fit our growing space and a little extra to give away and replace any casualties. As a result, we'd use fewer labels as well as fewer seed trays, pots, pest control products, seeds – and less compost. Investing in a few more expensive but lasting labels might be feasible if we are saving in other areas.

Seed Packets (and Seed Catalogues)

Use greaseproof paper or ordinary paper envelopes for your own saved seed, and as far as possible look for similar packaging when buying seed. Some suppliers mostly use paper packets (e.g. R Parsons Sweet Peas). Others, like The Real Seed Co. are moving to paper packets away from plastic ziplock bags for some varieties. Lobby your favourite suppliers to find alternatives to plastic for seed packaging and while you're doing that, ask them to stop using plastic sleeves for posting out seed catalogues. Some companies are changing to 'compostable plastic' catalogue sleeves, although there is some controversy over whether these plastics are any better.

As mentioned elsewhere in this guide, plastic films marketed as 'compostable' (e.g. compost bin liners, supermarket produce bags and said magazine covers) are often made with the addition of an accelerant ingredient (itself a substance of dubious environmental credentials) to make them biodegrade faster, which increases the release of greenhouse gases. In addition, these films can often only be composted in industrial composting processes – if you put them in your home compost bin, you'll be left with souvenir fragments to make you regret that moment of madness forever more. I often wonder why paper envelopes fell out of favour, but I guess clear plastic allows for advertising opportunities while the magazine is in transit. For those suppliers that are really stuck on their plastic catalogue covers, consider browsing their stock online instead and removing yourself from their mailing list.

- Seed balls or 'seed bombs' – soil-based balls with seed in, mostly for wildflower or floral species, and not likely to leave you with neatly sown rows, these won't replace all your seed needs. These balls have their origin in Guerrilla Gardening, a culture worth delving into if you like your rebellions subtle, scented and beautiful.

- Seed storing boxes – the good old Tupperware or sealable plastic food box is the go-to option for many people trying to keep their seed supplies in good nick from one season to the next. They are made of plastic, of course, but are hard to beat for their airtight properties. Instead, try using glass jars – maybe with a sheet of fabric or greaseproof paper trapped in the screw top thread to increase air- and water-tightness, in the time-honoured tradition of jam-makers. Some glass containers do now come with a silicone ring inside the lid which, when squashed hard between the rim of the jar and the metal lid, will form an airtight seal. Tin seed boxes are also on sale, and these could be a good option although they won't be free from humidity in the average shed or protect seed from temperature fluctuations.

Pegs

Congratulations on finding your biodegradable alternative to plastic-based fleece or mulch (see Crop Protection chapter), but what are you going to use to hold it in place in those situations where it's not feasible to use a heaped row of soil to weigh it down? Pegs – that's right. Sometimes they're made from metal or heavy-gauge wire, but many are made from … a big hunk of plastic.

Tildenet have created a peg they claim to be biodegradable. They certainly look like corn starch or similar and indeed their website says they're made from 100% biodegradable 'non-GM starch' so plant-based is about as near as we can get to knowing the actual source material. Other options are to use stones as weights to peg the crop covering fabric in place, make your own pegs from heavy-gauge fencing wire shaped into narrow, U-shaped hoops, or to use rough wooden pegs – perhaps split from offcuts or scrap wood.

Flower Arranging Oasis

For gardeners who like to make floral arrangements with their homegrown flower crops, there is a new floral foam that claims to be biodegradable, 'in biologically active landfill conditions'. The company is called Oasis Floral and the product is called Oasis Bio Floral Foam. They are a little vague about the materials used, saying only that they are 'sustainable' and that they have been tested by the American Society for Testing and Materials. They promise to provide updates on the progress of further testing. Take a look at their website if you'd like to know more.

Garden Kneelers

Kneelers offer cushioning to protect your knees during weeding or other work where you might be kneeling a lot or getting up and down frequently. Some of them are made from the same kind of foam that's used for swimming floats, while others might be constructed from an outer cover of plastic-coated cloth or neoprene stuffed with some kind of soft filling, possibly EVA foam. A third kind takes the form of a small plastic bench, a narrow cross strut supported on two extendable legs. One way up, it's a portable seat, turn it the other way and it's a kneeler with two 'arms' on which you can push yourself back up to standing. The final type that I know of are individual knee pads that you strap onto each leg. All of these common models will be made largely or entirely from plastic and polymer-based fabric. The only partially plastic-free design I could find was from Waitrose (no guarantees it will still be on their stock list) with a cover made of waxed cotton and leather. The filling, however, was very possibly foam – plastic to all intents and purposes.

I'm afraid the only option, if you're in the market for a new kneeler, may be to take the DIY route and fashion a cover from waxed cotton (for waterproofing) and a stuffing from some kind of soft and pliable material – an old cushion, or some unravelled wool or a worn-out woolly jumper. The quick and easy version would be to roll a sweater inside an old cagoule or waterproof jacket. Instant, waterproofed kneeling comfort.

Propagation Benches and Trays

In many climates, the growing season is short and keen gardeners rely on a little extra help to make the most of it. For those of us gardening in the colder latitudes of the temperate zones, it can be tricky to grow certain long season crops without a little 'bottom heat' to start seeds into action. By sprouting seedlings under protection in this way a month or two before you could safely sow direct outdoors, you can bring on young plants, getting a head start ready to fill the beds when the frosts are gone.

For this purpose, we have propagating benches (generally used in polytunnels or greenhouses) or windowsill propagators (mostly used in the home). The traditional propagating bench is a raised wooden tray filled with a layer of sand, over which a heating cable is laid in a regular wave pattern and in turn covered with more sand. This creates a warm bed for seed trays to sit on, mimicking the effect of gently warmed soil in spring: optimum sprouting conditions for seeds. The cable of a propagation bench, its plug and any dials that control it are likely to be plastic or plastic covered. A typical propagator is likely to give 20 years' service so would perhaps be justified on the grounds that it is a long-lasting plastic. When it is at the end of its useful life, it should be able to be recycled. Many local authorities have a separate collection area for 'Small Electrical Goods' which suggests there is a market for these materials, even if it is perhaps the copper wire and components inside rather than the plastic that is most lucrative for recycling.

For those without room for a greenhouse propagator, there are small heated units designed to fit on the typical domestic windowsill. These take the form of a narrow plastic tray with a heating cable coiled inside the topmost and bottom layers. Plug it in, set your seed trays or plant pots on top and, for about the same energy used by a light bulb, the tray will gently warm the compost and seeds and you should see germination in a matter of days. Once again, these propagators are likely to be used for several years and so can often be considered an investment purchase rather than a throwaway plastic product. The rigid plastic they're made of is indeed recyclable and there is a market for it, but as with many other items of similar construction, the devil is in the logistical detail. There is often no easy way for the average domestic consumer to have access to rigid plastics recycling streams. The companies that process these materials are at the high end of a chain that deals mostly with other large industry partners. If your local council has a recycling skip for small electricals, you could deposit your windowsill propagator there at the end of its useful life. If not, it could, with the cable removed, perhaps have a new life as a tray for containing and displaying house plants, whether on a windowsill or elsewhere.

For a more radical solution, consider taking inspiration from the Victorians whose competitive pineapple growing in 'hot beds' relied on tinkering with the heat-generating properties of composting ingredients stacked up under the growing beds. Poultry manure, straw and vegetable peelings all went into the mix, heaped up under a layer of soil. Today many gardeners practice varying hot bed techniques including the German tradition of 'Hügelkultur', heaped bed growing where dead wood and compost ingredients are piled up under soil to make a raised and soil-warming growing bed.

Some gardeners like to harness the heat-generating properties of their compost heap, a low-tech way of adding warmth to seed germination. Though the heat from composting will be less consistent and controlled than from an electric propagator, it's perhaps an interesting area to experiment with since the heat from the heap is free. In the chapter on Composting, there is some mention of how 'hot-box' composting methods can speed up the process of turning raw waste materials into compost. By deploying various tweaks to accelerate the feverish microbial procreation and respiration processes that drive any compost heap, you are also likely to increase the heat generated. The most basic way to make use of this heat might be to place seed trays on top of the compost heap. There are no guarantees that this will work, since it involves natural processes and imprecise proportions of raw materials, but it might be fun to try.

Avoid	Try
Plastic plant labels.	Slate, wood, bamboo, clay or metal alternatives.
Plastic tools.	Wood and metal traditional designs.

4

CROP PROTECTION

We have all grown so used to our cloche tunnels and domes, fleece, netting, weed suppressing membranes, weed sprays, bug potions, little plastic cold frames and greenhouses. It seemed like a tall order to find substitutes for them all. But lo, dear green-fingered reader, I think we've done it – almost.

COVERS, CLOCHES, TUNNELS AND MEMBRANES

Weed Suppressing Membranes and Fabrics

Black woven landscaping fabric just doesn't go away; you may have noticed this when stray fibres escape and can be found fluttering on a fence wire years after you laid the stuff. Made typically from polypropylene, which is manufactured from propene, a by-product of fossil fuel extraction, these geotextiles are designed to suppress weeds by blocking light but are permeable to allow gases and liquids to pass through them. They are designed to be long-lasting and sturdy, which is why you can find frayed threads from the cut edges hanging around for years.

Polypropylene is eminently recyclable. The trouble with weed-suppressing membrane is that it is woven from long thin strips of thin polypropylene to make a textile that can be easily laid over the contours of the earth. These 'threads' when they separate are not easy to capture and put in the right recycling bin. The textiles tend to be ingrained with mud after use and this further reduces their chances of being recycled. But you could consider other ways of keeping weeds down.

Newspaper and Cardboard

Try layers of cardboard or several layers of newspaper, covered over with compost or bark mulch. They can be moulded to fit the shape of the soil underneath if dampened. These won't last as long, only a year or so before breaking down, but will give you a weed-free season or two. The traditional way to block weeds out on a fallow bed was to lay old carpet over the soil. This is great if the carpet is wool and has a biodegradable backing, as it will break down slowly. But many carpets today are made from nylons and synthetic fibre mixes with some plastic in their backing weave and glue. These may take decades to break down and will mix lots of microfibres into your soil when they do, so are perhaps not such a great alternative.

Biodegradable Custom Membranes

Corn-starch fabric and biodegradable weed-control fabrics like DeWitt natural weed-barrier (cellulose based) can be very effective and, a bit like the layers of newspaper mentioned above, can be prettied up with mulches on top such as grass clippings, cocoa shell mulch (toxic to pets if they eat it), bark chips or pine needle mulch. But these will also be short term weed-suppressing fixes as they will all break down over a season or two. However, by suppressing a year or two's worth of weed seed and putting a layer between your soil and any seeds falling onto it from plants and passing birds and animals, you will reduce the amount of viable weed seed in your garden soil seed bank.

On a smaller scale, you can find wool, hemp and jute mats and mulches to help suppress weeds in small areas. Mulches like this should have the bonus effect of reducing the need for watering (water and feed plants well before laying any mulch, and don't mulch when the soil is icy as you can trap the ice in for months and slow the soil's warming in spring). These mats will biodegrade after 18 months to three years. Such options tend to be more appropriate for single containers or around specimen plants as they're small. The Woolly Shepherd uses UK sheep fleeces that may otherwise be wasted because of their dark colour and hence lower value. They sell various products including The Garden Square, a 50cm square piece of felted wool that can be cut to size to fit a pot or the area around a plant. Similarly, jute mats are available from The Chimney Sheep among other suppliers.

WeedGuardPlus, sold by Mulch Organic in the UK, was originally developed for US growers, mainly larger commercial customers, but is now available to small, domestic scale gardeners. It's a cellulose-based membrane sold in rolls that can be manually or machine laid and includes options with holes in to accommodate seeds or young plants laid out in regular grid and line formations. It lasts one growing season before biodegrading. Different products from the same supplier are designed for polytunnel or outdoor use. Mulch Organic also offer heavy-duty corn starch sheets, pre-cut, that can be used for individual shrubs or specimen plants and can last up to three years. Among their more interesting products are biodegradable sheet mulches impregnated with fertilizers and specific minerals so theoretically you can suppress weeds and feed your crops with one product.

Gravel and Stone Mulches

If gravel is laid in a thick enough layer, most weed seeds will not be able to germinate through it, so negating the need for a plastic geotextile layer underneath. Aim for a minimum of four inches (10 cm). But do be careful to clear the ground of any perennial weeds already rooted in the area first as they will be able to thrust through a thick gravel mulch over time. Disadvantages of laying gravel or stone mulches without a geotextile fabric underneath is that the stones may sink into the earth, so periodic replenishment may be needed, and they can be more difficult to remove later. Or you could start with a cellulose or paper mulch layer as a base, keeping the gravel separate from the soil for the first year or two at least.

Cloches

Use glass in place of plastic to protect individual plants. Small glass bell cloches can be purchased cheaply. They will last far longer than plastic ones: with a bit of a scrub at the end of the season to remove any algae or soil, they'll be good to go again in the spring. Large jam or pickle jars make fine improvised cloches. The weight of glass cloches generally helps keep them in place whereas plastic varieties need pegs (plastic or metal) to stand their ground in windy or stormy conditions. Finally, plastic covers can become opaque over time with sun exposure, further reducing their useful lifespan. Glass remains clear for centuries.

Crop Protection Tunnels and Frames

Tunnels to protect individual rows and groups of plants have tended to be made from plastics, but it wasn't always that way. Fleece, especially of the cheaper, thinner grades, tends to break into useless pieces after a season or two of exposure to the weather, once again demonstrating the false economy and short-lived convenience of many plastic products. Instead you could use glass frames, a larger version of the cloche with several panes, like the Victorians did. Their classic designs are still replicated today (tent style, or more elaborate mini-greenhouse shapes) and can be dropped over individual plants, rows or group plantings. Of course, these are more expensive than a roll of fleece, but they will last for many years and won't pollute your neighbour's garden and your own with hundreds of tiny cloud-like fragments.

You can also use individual panes of spare glass propped up with a brick. Another option is to make some DIY portable frames to place over plants from old window frames. There are books and websites with designs and ideas for hundreds of different ways of doing this, depending on your level of skill and the kind of leftover materials you have to work with.

Polytunnels

No alternatives to the polythene covered polytunnel emerged from my current searches, apart from using glass green-houses. Given they may need re-skinned every five years or so (ten if you read the promotional literature of polytunnel suppliers), more frequently in stormy years or where vandalism is a problem, polytunnels are not quite single-use plastics, but neither are they so long-lasting as to negate any worries about the disposal of the old coverings. Suppliers say that companies can be found who will recycle worn out poly-tunnel skins and the type of plastic used can be readily repro-cessed. Indeed, there are companies that recycle polytunnel skins, but the majority seem to cater to farms and other larger businesses so it's not clear how a domestic gardener would send their old tunnel polythene for recycling. The suppliers further argue that by growing your own food and cutting your carbon footprint that way, the polythene tunnel is still a sustainable choice, if you weigh up a broader bunch of envi-ronmental impact measures.

It's not an entirely compelling argument, as small-scale local food production has very different carbon inputs and outputs (not always less carbon heavy than the most efficient commercial producers especially when you consider the scale, costs and speed of each system as a whole) and not all food we buy is airfreighted or transported in terribly polluting ways. Perhaps if you really want to avoid plastic but don't have the money for a new glass greenhouse, a middle way would be to look for a second-hand greenhouse.

A polytunnel that is efficiently used, cropping all year round, carefully maintained and protected from the worst storm damage, repaired and patched as needed, could still be a justifiable choice. If, when the time comes to replace the skin, it is taken to an appropriate recycling plant, most of the concerns about plastic's environmental costs will have been carefully minimised. Perhaps it's worth asking tunnel suppliers about recycling before purchasing: are they able to take back the cover for recycling? If not, which recycler would they recommend that will accept old tunnel covers from individual home growers? If nothing else, this will remind polytunnel suppliers of their customers' concern for the sustainability of materials they buy.

It would be wonderful to see polytunnel manufacturers and recycling companies working closely together to create an easy-to-access closed loop for domestic growers to reprocess plastic tunnel skins; that would go a long way to reducing concerns about the environmental impact of growing tunnels.

Polycarbonate Greenhouses and Cold Frames

Use toughened horticultural glass instead of polycarbonate where possible. Cold frames and greenhouses can be improvised using unwanted glass and old windows, though these won't typically be made from the toughened glass that is best for garden use. Polycarbonate grows opaque over time with sunlight exposure, though treated and coated panels can be found that are said to resist UV degradation for longer. It's perhaps another area in which to reconsider our traditional approaches to gardening and go back to the fundamentals of how and why we garden. Making a list of pros and cons and noting down the reasons for wanting a greenhouse or cold frame will provide a good starting point for considering alternatives. Some people, including some very well-known gardeners, have eschewed greenhouses and use a potting shed for raising seedlings and protecting tender plants or clear a space in a garage with a large window.

Could you fulfil the aspirations you had for a greenhouse or cold frame by making or expanding a large south or east facing window in an existing shed or outbuilding with a shelf or table in front of it? Could you use windowsills in the house for bringing on tender plants? Or is there a workroom space you could use for potting work in inclement weather? Alternatively, could you change the crops you want to grow and do without a greenhouse? Consider the footprint of a poly-tunnel or greenhouse – what else could you use the space for? Other ideas may emerge that are more appealing than a greenhouse.

If you decide a greenhouse is a must and find that polycarbonate ones are the only kind that fit your budget, try to think through how you will recycle the materials when they are no longer functional. There is a market for polycarbonate recycling, and it would be a useful exercise to ask suppliers of polycarbonate greenhouses how they suggest their product can be recycled at the end of its useful life. As government requirements increasingly put the responsibility on manufacturers to reduce waste and increase the recycling potential of their products, they will develop more helpful information for such questions from prospective buyers.

Planting Styles and Systems

It's possible to provide some protection and support to crops by planting other species nearby that will confuse or distract pests, attract pollinators or act as a windbreak. Some of these principles are followed by permaculture adherents and websites or books covering this area may be a source of plant combination ideas. One obvious and time-honoured example is to plant a climbing rose or clematis beside a tree so the climbing plant can use the trunk and branches for support. Another classic is to plant willow 'fedge' as a windbreak to protect more vulnerable plants until they become established. (A fedge is a cross between a hedge and a fence, made by spearing a line of willow wands into the ground: as they grow, the branches are woven together forming a latticework. A fedge needs diligent annual maintenance to keep it within its allocated space.)

The garden writer Alys Fowler is a fan of 'polyculture', where different crops are planted in a mix in the same area or bed. This is thought to have advantages over the traditional crop rotation approach with rows of single crops from the same family in separate beds. By planting alliums, brassicas and root vegetables intermingled in the same bed, it's theoretically harder for pests e.g. carrot fly to home in on their target plant, because the scents of other plants confuse them and create other deterrents. For example, the large leafy structure of brassicas might present a physical barrier stopping flies getting close enough to lay their eggs by the carrot seedlings.

Fleece

Fleece, not to be confused with the coloured microfibre garments that many gardeners wear (see the chapter on clothing), is used to keep pests and frost off tender crops. It's made from polyester or polypropylene, synthetic polymer-based materials. We've become used to seeing long white stretches of it covering furrows across the countryside and equally to casting smaller lengths of it over our most prized seedlings on nights when low temperatures still threaten to bite. Some gardeners use fleece fabric over hoops to make cloche tunnels to cover crop rows. Fleece serves a very useful protective purpose in our gardens, but it is prone to degrading quickly when exposed to the elements – and to flaking into thousands of pieces as it does so. The better-quality brands are thicker and longer lasting. To cut this kind of plastic from our gardens, I can see two options. One is to change your gardening methods so that you don't need it, sowing only when the threat of frost is past and using other pest deterrent methods to protect against carrot root fly and others. The other option is to find an alternative product that isn't made from plastic.

Hessian seems to be the main alternative to polypropylene fleece offered on the UK market. A 200gsm weave weight is typically sold to wrap around or lay over tender plants to protect from cold. Other gardeners have used old net curtains to protect crops. Although these are typically made from synthetic fibres, if they are being thrown out to landfill anyway, and there's a vacancy for a fleece-like fabric in your garden crop protection armoury, they should last a good while longer than the white horticultural fleece fabrics. You could make frames or cloche-like covers by stretching net curtains over wooden or wire structures. These could be dropped over particular crops when the need for protection arises.

Rhubarb Forcers

Buy a clay one instead of using an upturned plastic bucket. Or use a large, upturned flowerpot with a flat stone placed over the drainage hole to block out light, or a zinc or enamelled tin bucket, perhaps weighted down with a stone.

SPRAYS, PELLETS AND POTIONS

Most weed killers and insecticides, and many fertilizers and soil conditioners like lime, come in plastic bottles or tubs. There are some good reasons for this. Often they are prone to absorbing moisture from the air and so need to be in a semi-airtight container or they're corrosive and must be securely packaged. But in some cases, there is no real need for a plastic package.

As ever, the first line of defence is to use home-made alternatives or buy the fertilizer or additive in cardboard containers (where there's a choice) or in bulk to reduce the amount of plastic packaging. When buying fertilizer in bulk, be careful not to buy more than you (and any gardeners you'll be sharing it with) can use before the expiry date. Always make good use of the chance to give customer feedback to the seller on how they could improve their business by reducing plastic.

Feeds

From foliar feeds sprayed on from a bottle to pelleted fertilizer sold in a tub to concentrates that you dilute and apply from a watering can, many plant feeds and fertilizers come in plastic bottles or tubs. With liquid products this is tricky; cardboard is clearly not an option. But at least one famous plant food brand, Baby Bio, used to come in a glass bottle. I remember it quite vividly for some reason, a small bulbous bottle of dark brown concentrate with a long thin neck. It lived under the sink in our house and would be brought out to share around the houseplants in carefully measured, diluted doses. A tiny bottle would last a long time because it was so concentrated. It's not easy to tell from the pictures online whether the Baby Bio bottle is still made of glass but you can see that it now comes wrapped in plastic film – what a shame. It would be nice to think more plant food companies could revert to glass packaging in time and with enough consumer pressure.

There are arguments that glass is not such a wonder product, from the perspective of environmental sustainability. It can be heavy to transport and requires a certain amount of fuel and energy to clean, recycle and make back into more glass bottles or jars. But in this particular area of garden feeds, where plastic vessels would possibly not be accepted in kerbside recycling, glass looks like a promising option to improve recycling potential and cut waste. Get busy with your emails to the manufacturers and vote with your wallet wherever you see glass-packaged options.

Otherwise, buy feed in bulk sizes to improve the packaging-to-product ratio and in clear plastic containers where possible to improve the chances that the packaging can be recycled. Opaque, coloured plastics often have a lower recycling value.

DIY Fertilizers

One more practical solution is to make your own fertilizers and plant food. Steeping nettle or comfrey leaves in a covered bucket of water for a few weeks will make a potent (and very smelly), nitrogen-rich feed that you can dilute and apply to most crops. Some gardeners also use a small amount of manure left to soak in a bucket of water to make a liquid feed in a similar way.

Applying a mulch of manure (collected from a farm or stables) or garden compost will provide a good all-round fertilizer as well as boosting the microbial life of the soil.

Seaweed

Seaweed is one of the most popular plant feeds among gardeners. Most seaweed sold for horticultural use is Ascophyllum nodosum, known in the UK and the US as knotted wrack. It's common on sheltered rocky shores and is confined to the North Atlantic Ocean.

Research evidence, and there's a stack of it, suggests that seaweeds contain a surprising number of minerals that plants can use to boost their growth. Data from many studies also show that seaweed feeds seem to be associated with increased plant resilience and immunity. While seaweed is not a complete food – it can't substitute compost or manure, for instance – it is a very useful supplement with benefits whose mechanisms are still not completely understood. People who live near beaches may be able to collect seaweed to use as a fertilizer/soil additive, depending on local permissions. While seaweed collection to improve the soil has a long tradition in coastal areas of Ireland, Scotland and the Northern US, many coastal regions are subject to laws prohibiting the removal of any natural materials from their shores, so always check with the relevant council department.

Some local authorities themselves gather seaweed from beaches for various reasons and may allow local people to take limited amounts for domestic garden use. Seaweed should only ever be gathered from the beach when it has been washed up by the tide, and never from the water or close to the waterline, where it may still be attached to rocks and providing food and habitat for sea creatures. Follow precautions to rinse or stack the seaweed for a while to remove salt before putting it on the garden.

For those of us not lucky enough to live by the sea, there are many seaweed preparations on the market. Unfortunately, many of these are liquid formulations – concentrated seaweed liquors that come in plastic containers. Some sellers also offer seaweed meal or powder, and these are dry, shredded or milled products that in some cases are sold in card or metal packaging, though beware, many also come in plastic pouch packs which are not recyclable. You can then work the meal into the soil or steep it or mix powder formulae with water to make a liquid feed. There are also some online videos explaining how to use edible dried seaweed products (dried, not roasted) to make your own liquid preparations. These involve water and a blender. It's not clear whether these home-made seaweed smoothies have the same nutritional value as the seaweed offered for horticultural use, or are the same species, but perhaps it's worth running your own trials?

Crop Rotation

Arguably, if you practice good garden hygiene techniques, clearing away diseased material (burn or put in the general waste bins, not your home composter) and operating a good crop rotation system, you may not need to use any additional feeds or fertilizers. In a typical crop rotation scheme, you'll grow plants from the same botanical family together in one bed and then rotate crops to a new bed each year, applying manure or compost to the beds where you'll plant the greediest feeders, like brassicas. The main idea behind rotation is to prevent pests building up in one area. If you grow the same crop year after year in the same spot, you're likely to get a problem with pests that specifically attack that crop/family e.g. their larvae getting established in the top layer of soil ready to decimate the young plants you put in next year. But if you rotate, the pests, such as cabbage root fly, will find it's now alliums growing in the place where broccoli was last year, and the voracious tribe will have to start again in a new bed.

Some of the crops in a rotation may also help nourish the crop that follows them next year, so for example beans, peas and other legumes may leave their nitrogen fixing root nodules for the heavy feeding brassicas that are planted after them (don't pull the beans out but instead snip the stems at ground level, leaving the roots in the ground) although the evidence that this has any significant effect is patchy. Potato crops are said to 'clean' their area of the plot as their large leaves block out light and suppress weeds.

If you manure a vegetable bed in autumn, it should not, except in special cases, need extra fertilizers added during the growing season. Similarly, with ornamentals, often simply top-dressing plants with a layer of compost or well-rotted manure will provide all the nutrients they need, and potentially in a more balanced and readily available form than packaged fertilizers. Soil and compost top dressings will also add beneficial fungi and bacteria not available from packeted fertilizers that plants will appreciate.

Pest Control

Try bio-controls (typically supplied by mail order as strange flossy powders, smears of dark scales on card or as individual pupae or larvae to be placed at the base of plants). Some are mixed with water in a watering can and poured onto the soil, others are hung from the plant leaves. Timing is important to allow populations to multiply and feed on the target pest at the right stage in their life cycle. Or try home-made deterrents such as soap spray (in a brass or glass sprayer).

A blast of water from the hose can be enough to keep some pests in check, such as certain aphids. This may need to be done regularly and the vigilant gardener will get best results by noticing infestations early and taking action. Blasting with the hose can be damaging for some foliage and young tender plants, so use discerningly. Diligent torchlit slug patrols may be as effective as pellets from a plastic tub.

Some gardeners take a whole-ecosystem view, leaving certain pest populations as food for other species such as birds. This school of pest control comes from seeing the garden in the round, including all the species that live there or visit and weighing up the likely damage from pests – for instance, aphids (distortion of leaves, slight unsightliness, possible virus transmission) – against the benefits of providing food for blue tits and other species. It might require patience and a whole new mindset but there are lots of ideas and information out there to guide you on this route. Start with BBC's *Springwatch: Wild in the Garden* series with Kate Bradbury, on iPlayer.

Reconfigure the layouts of beds. For example, if grass edging or wooden battens are providing a haven for slugs, use metal edging, woven hurdle edges or neatly clipped grass boundaries with a cleanly cut gap between the grass and the heaped-up soil of the bed. Regular re-edging will help keep the beds looking neat as well as reducing slug hiding places.

Try copper tape around pots: it's said slugs don't like that. You can also try it around wooden bed edges, if you have enough.

Encourage birds, frogs and beneficial insects into your garden. They will provide pest-control services in return for some cosy habitat and fodder. This might include building a pond, or just sinking a biscuit tin or dustbin lid into the ground, making hibernacula, or heaping up some stones or dead wood in a corner to shelter insects or frogs, planting food plants to provide lots of nectar and pollen, and increasing your tolerance for weeds, at least in a small area of the garden.

Avoid	Try
Geotextile membranes and fleece.	Hessian plant covers. Gravel and bark mulches.
Fertilizers in plastic tubs and bottles.	Crop Rotation. Make your own DIY liquid fertilizers and compost.
Insecticides in plastic bottles.	Bio-controls and polyculture.

5

PLANT SUPPORTS

Some plants, while they may be quite happy to grow scrambling around on the earth, will need some kind of propping up if they are to grow in the way we gardeners desire. Many climbing plants have developed to grow through the branches of a tree, for example, and would do exactly this in their native habitat. But we can't always supply a tree of suitable proportions in the middle of a suburban plot. So if we want our roses to be nicely displayed, covering an unsightly fence, maybe, and if we wish the blooms to be easy to sniff or cut for the vase, and want to be able to pick French beans easily, we need to put in a proxy tree. Some of the products sold to support plants are plastic, despite there being a good range of non-plastic options. Read on for the alternatives.

Netting

Bean and pea netting is often made from bright green plastic, but there are options now made from string or jute twine. Jute alternatives are becoming gradually more available and can look attractive, blending into the garden better than the garish tones of plastic netting. As with many other plastic garden materials like fleece and plant labels, plastic netting will partially degrade when exposed to the elements, becoming brittle and breaking up. With cheaper products, this often happens within a couple of seasons. While we often talk about biodegradability as a desirable quality of garden materials, the problem with plastic items like netting is that they only degrade so far, into small fragments that render them useless for their intended purpose. And since they are impossible to recycle in this state, these fragments then become thousands of little pieces of environmental litter.

The raw materials in your compost bin after being digested and processed by bacteria, fungi and worms, break down into their constituent elements, undergoing a complete transformation in appearance, chemical structure and physical properties. The raw materials we put into a compost heap (banana skins, carrot peelings, coffee filter papers) look and behave entirely differently at the start of the process compared with at the end (rich, dark brown friable compost). At the end of their metamorphosis, what started off as leftover crusts and vegetable peelings have become a rich humus that can help bind soil, release nutrients to be taken up again by plants and put to good use in biological and environmental cycles, stimulate worm activity and improve soil structure.

Pieces of plastic netting, on the other hand, like fleece and plant labels, won't change. Instead, their basic physical properties and chemical make-up will endure largely unchanged except in size and integrity. Plastics, instead of breaking down into new compounds that might be usefully absorbed by natural cycles of decay, will carry on disintegrating into small and then tiny pieces but persisting for decades, even centuries, as microplastics, lingering in landfill or perhaps being blown down a drain and finding their way into the sea or a fatberg.

Bamboo Canes

Most gardeners already rely on bamboo canes for some jobs. They are a renewable way to stake plants that need support, as are stakes coppiced from hazel, birch, willow and other trees, while dowelling and short sticks may be used for smaller plants. Consider, if you have the room, growing your own hazel or willow for the express purpose of providing staking material. One or two small, hedge height plants are all you might need for a small plot, and with regular coppicing, they need never outgrow their allotted space. Tie the stakes into structures, tepees, lines and more elaborate designs using string, wire, raffia, wool and even the twigs of whippy growth from branches of birch and willow.

Resist the offers from companies who want to sell you plastic caps, balls and other 'systems' for holding your bamboo canes together. You can find terracotta or oak cane toppers in some garden centres or suppliers such as Nutscene and you may be able to think of creative alternatives: hollowed-out corks, metal screw tops from wine or water bottles, squashed and moulded to fit around the canes. Used latex or rubber gloves could be bound over cane tops with rubber bands, as could small pieces of fabric. Some gardeners use small upturned terracotta plant pots which can look very attractive, or upturned glass bottles (clear or coloured glass or painted inside, if you like the effect and have the time). Bottles and pots are a good option if you want not only to make sharp cane tops less of a hazard to gardeners' eyes but also to support protecting covers like netting; canes alone would poke through the netting and puncture more solid materials like fleece.

Plant Ties

Shred old clothes and other textiles for plant ties. Fabric offcuts are soft and pliable yet durable and will make excellent material for securing espaliered trees to trellises and bean plants to tepee frameworks, and for training grape vines, roses etc.

Good old-fashioned twine, string and raffia are made from biodegradable, plant-based materials. Avoid plastic-coated wire ties. See the Sundries section in the Tools and Equipment chapter for more on this.

Workarounds

Grow dwarf/bush varieties of beans, tomatoes and squashes, and even 'tumbler' tomato varieties that will trail down from a tall chimney pot or hanging planter, thus eliminating the need to support plants at all. In the greenhouse, it's possible to use twine suspended from the roof struts and wound round plant stalks to support cordon tomatoes and other crops such as squash and vines.

Try growing mixed planting, particularly perennials and shrubs, where the structure of one plant supports another. For instance, a tall Veronicastrum or fennel and some upright grasses such as Stipa arundinacea (Anemanthele), Miscanthus or varieties of Calamagrostis might work well to support more delicate creatures like Gypsophila which otherwise might flop over, especially after heavy rain.

In a similar vein, look into 'Three Sisters' edible crop planting styles, originating in Mexico and said to be used over centuries by Iroquois farmers among other groups. A sweet-corn plant, or a cluster of them (tall and rigid) supports a bean plant or two clambering up the stem(s) and a pumpkin or winter squash plant scrambles around on the soil below, suppressing weeds and retaining soil moisture with its broad leaves. The beans are not heavy feeders and in fact their nitrogen fixing roots may help to enrich the soil for the other two crops. The lesson is simple: use the natural structure and habit of one plant to support others that thrive and can co-exist happily in similar conditions. Get creative and invent your own mutually supportive combinations. The main criterion is that the plants must be compatible and like similar conditions and cultivation approaches. If you plant cucumbers with tomatoes for instance, there's a chance they might not get along too well as tomatoes like dry, hot conditions while cucumbers prefer lots of watering and high humidity.

If your main gardening technique is neglect (I'm not thinking of anyone in particular at the Trellis Potting Shed), no problem, but combine plants that all tolerate neglect or indeed thrive in such conditions. Mediterranean herbs are one good example for poor soil in areas with a decent amount of sunshine. If you plant something thuggish that will take over any spare square inch of soil with delicate, tender specimens that need pampering, there's only going to be one winner and your Three Sisters will soon become a rather lonely one.

For more permanent planting, you may have seen examples of clematis or rambling roses climbing through established trees or shrubs to stunning effect. The blossoms of the rose or clematis are enhanced against the darker green background of the tree canopy and their stems are happily supported by the tree's sturdy framework.

Similarly, trees under-planted with early bulbs often work well as the bulb species can make use of the light and irrigation through the bare branches (of deciduous trees) in winter and then are protected from the strongest sun of summer when the tree is in full leaf. Under-planting combinations in summer might use mid-height perennials such as salvias, nepetas or geraniums to hide the 'legs' of climbing roses or other tall plants. Once again, the mid-height plants will help suppress weeds and complement the visual appeal of the roses, fitting into a niche left by the climbing habit of the taller plant, which will tend to branch and flower only from above its first meter or so of growth. The medium perennials may 'lean' a little on the rose stems for support.

You can achieve some interesting effects by planting two different sorts of climbers together, allowing one to take advantage of the supporting role of the other. One example would be to combine woody, rigid climbers such as roses with floppy climbers that require support such as jasmine or clematis. While you still probably need a trellis or wires for training the rose, the clematis could make its own way up the limbs of the rose. With careful selection, it's possible to create a stunning, complementary display where the rose and clematis blooming seasons coincide, or a long season of interest where one flowers after the other has finished.

With some plants that would usually need support, try growing them as trailers or scramblers survival-of-the-fittest style. Some roses, clematis and other plants with a trailing, spreading nature will work well as handsome ground cover if left to run over the soil. I've seen Thunbergia grown as a dangling trailer from manger planters or hanging baskets, cascading in a very appealing, natural looking form. In fact, it might be said that it looks happier this way, with its stems allowed to twist and droop, seeking out the next tussock of grass or branch to cling to, as it might do in the forest edges, riverbanks and scrublands of its native East Africa. Grown in this way, other plants fill out Thunbergia's typically sparse growth habit, making for a more attractive display than when it's grown all alone, pinioned to a suburban trellis, in what is often an underwhelmingly meagre display.

Metal or Wire Supports

You can buy or make metal frames to support plants with a floppy or swooning growth habit, and you won't need a blacksmith's workshop to make some very simple plant frames from metal. Monty Don makes semi-circular supports by bending a curve in the centre section of lengths of iron rebar, then bending the two end sections downwards through a 90° angle. The ends are then driven into the soil. The final structure looks like two legs joined in a horizontal bowing curve at the top, forming a gentle prop for plants to lean against. Garden retailers sell plant stakes in all manner of different shapes and designs tailored to plants of every size and habit growing in all kinds of situation. There are different metals to choose from too.

Some of the simplest designs are traditional metal vine eyes and vine hooks that can be wiggled into mortar or screwed into timber posts and linked with wire or twine to support everything from temporary annual climbers to more permanent plantings like fan-trained fruit trees.

Another option might be to pinch out plants that are likely to have a floppy growth habit to make them bushier and shorter. You may not completely do away with the need for support, but the plants will be stockier and may even flower more as a bonus.

Repurpose old ladders, fence panels, bed frames, bicycle wheels and other frames as plant supports. You may find some creative and functional ideas come from experimenting with materials that are no longer needed for their original purpose. A gardener I know reckons the sides of a baby's cot, with the base removed, makes an excellent plant support.

Some designs are more decorative and practical than others, but there's a lot of fun to be had in trying out materials in different situations, and often at no cost except your time. I have seen an old lampshade frame, fabric removed, pegged upside down into the soil as a vase-style plant support for dahlias and penstemons. Other clever gardeners or perhaps garden magazine stylists have adapted a bicycle wheel, hung from a balcony or pergola roof with a climber tangling through it, to make a kind of botanical chandelier.

Make or buy wooden obelisks and trellis structures. This can be an enjoyable and rewarding DIY craft project and you can find lots of instructions online. If you choose treated wood and paint the structures well, the results will be long lasting. You can use up scrap wood in this way, adapting designs to suit what you have.

Avoid	Try
Plastic nets and stakes.	Bamboo, hazel and willow stakes, twine, and planting combinations that make use of the upright habit of other plants.
Plastic-coated wire ties.	Fabric ties, string and twine.

6

GARDEN ORNAMENTS, FURNITURE AND HARD LANDSCAPING

Take a look at any garden programme on TV or magazine gardening feature and you'll have a good chance of spotting some images of plastic: sofas, waterproof cushions, decking and blocks for building beds and walls made of plastics, artfully arranged with plastic flower and butterfly ornaments and fairy lights. The number of products for garden entertaining and leisure hitting the mass market lately seems to have exploded. You can buy coloured spirals that turn in the wind and catch the light, plastic sculptures and bird boxes, PVC bunting to decorate your shed and plastic weathervanes to embellish the shed roof. More plastic garden ornaments and 'outdoor room' accoutrements than you ever knew you needed. There are also, increasingly, plastic plants for sale, from table decorations to bouquets to plastic 'plant' tiles to make 'green' walls. Dare we also mention artificial turf (formerly known as Astro-Turf), that most controversial of products? We'll come to that in the Landscaping section.

There are perhaps too many varieties in this category to do them all justice here but let's focus on a few of the more common items and try to figure out some pointers and general principles that should help navigate the rest.

ORNAMENTS

I'm not going to be a spoilsport here; I like a tasteful garden bauble as much as the next person. But happily, there are metal options, wood, glass and ceramic too. You can make your own, without requiring too much natural talent, and craft books and magazines as well as websites like Pinterest will provide you with an almost infinite font of inspiration. Simple projects include making garlands, heart-shaped or circular, from sliced up or whole wine corks threaded onto wire, or grapevines fashioned into wreaths then embellished with dried flowers, seed heads and foliage. Other wreath-style decorations are made by wiring sturdy twigs together into shapes: sunbursts, fish, stars, that can be hung on fences or sheds. Bamboo stake ornaments are another entry-level project to consider. Simple painted canes, stuck in the soil in artful arrangements, can make an attractive feature.

At certain therapeutic gardening projects, I've seen a slightly more elaborate version of this with only a small increase in effort: bamboo canes topped with (coloured, plain or painted) glass bottles or jars upended on the tops of canes. These add punctuations of colour and height to a border and the glass reflects light, but they can also earn their keep by working as cane toppers and plant or netting supports. For a slightly more elaborate bamboo stake project, make small lanterns (jars with candle stubs or tea-lights inside set on a handful of sand or grit), suspended from bamboo canes by a handle of wire wrapped around the neck of the jar beneath the screw-top ridges. The wire is looped over the top and secured with another turn or two around the jar neck.

Fabric bunting is widely available. No need to buy plastic. You can make your own from offcuts of cotton and other fabrics, perhaps leftover from making curtains or mending clothes or deckchairs. Or use worn out, recycled household linens: sheets, tablecloths, napkins. Cut the fabric into isosceles triangles (this is the moment your school geometry notes come into their own) of the same size and attach the short edge to a long string or ribbon by doubling it over the ribbon and either stitching, stapling or gluing each flag in place. Don't forget to leave a length at each end for tying the bunting to a post or tree. Knitters can make knitted bunting. You can also buy ready-made fabric bunting in many garden centres.

PLASTIC PLANTS AND FLOWERS

My objections to plastic plants are many and include their often poor quality, unconvincing colours and forms, their unchanging nature (due to being lifeless) a direct inversion of one of the most loveable properties of real plants, their lack of scent and tactile qualities, and their tendency to collect dust and other debris. That's not to say, however, that I can't appreciate the reasons why some people value them. Artificial plants never wilt, so they keep their colour, structure and blooms all year round, and they're low maintenance in so far as they don't need watering, feeding or repotting (although they may need dusting). They are not fussy about where you place them, so you can put a fern on a bright windowsill and a sun-loving cactus or Mediterranean plant in a dark bathroom or study. And they are everlasting: buy them once and that plant will adorn its chosen spot for years. Some very well-made plants can be admired for their artistry (sincerely).

The quality of artificial plants is getting better – in some respects, at least. I used to pride myself on being able to spot a fake plant at 50 paces, but it's getting trickier now. Artificial plants of a certain vintage, or of lower quality, will often have a tell-tale blue-ish tinge to the green of their leaves, or a garish, shiny finish to their plastic sepals and leaf ribs. Rigid parts such as stems and stamens may have clumsily finished edges, rough seams of plastic that betray the moulds they came out of, or fraying edges on fabric petals. Modern artificial plants, however, are leagues apart from their ungainly forebears. These days, there is less to distinguish the fakes from the real deal, at least in passing, and when you don't have a live specimen to compare. There are some impressive silk flowers and plants on the market that, even if their main aim is not verisimilitude, are attractive and far more elegant than the brash specimens of old. But good quality silk plants will be expensive, and they may still include some plastic components in the stem or the centre of flowers, or on leaf ribs.

The majority of artificial plants are still made using quite a lot of plastic: some indeed are 100% plastic, while others use plastics for stems and flower centres, and sometimes for the 'earth' in which they are 'planted'. If the leaves and petals are not plastic, most likely they'll be made from a synthetic textile such as acrylic or nylon, non-biodegradable and a potential source of microfibres. Not to put too fine a point on it, artificial plants such as these would not be a good choice for anyone aiming to reduce their reliance on plastic.

A minority of artificial flowers are made from plant materials such as corn cob leaves. These would be entirely compostable, assuming they have not been varnished or sealed with some plastic-based paint.

There has been a trend over the last few years for making giant 'pom-pom' flowers from layers of folded tissue paper as an ephemeral home or garden/gazebo decoration. These are compostable, cheap and plastic-free and can be made to suit your décor or a friend's favourite colours. I have also seen a couple of contemporary artists creating breathtakingly detailed giant paper flowers with a realism and intricacy that elevates the form to something akin to sculpture. Artists such as Tiffanie Turner are paving the way, perhaps, for a more sustainable form of artificial flower. Look out for her work at a gallery near you.

GARDEN SEATING

Simple seating, benches and chairs, unadorned, are a relatively easy area in which to avoid plastic: lots of metal and wood options are on offer and they just need a little TLC, oiling and repainting now and then. The garden furniture industry has developed way beyond this in recent years, however, so we must take a more in-depth look at the many options.

'OUTDOOR ROOM' FURNITURE

Once upon a time, garden seating meant a wooden, or cast iron and wood bench, not prized for its plushness and comfort but perfectly serviceable, particularly when it was given a ceremonial scrub down and a lick of paint now and then. It could also include a kitchen chair brought out to the lawn on hot days and a few creaking deckchairs, hauled out of the shed, lightly cobwebbed, to cradle us through another summer. The garden furniture market has expanded stratospherically from those simple times, and you can choose from a bewildering array of sofas, armchairs, footstools, recliners, fixed and free-standing hammocks, daybeds, loungers and elaborately finished chaise-longues. This aspirational market can match the sophistication of indoor furniture, so corner sofas and three-piece suites that could take up a fair chunk of your patio or lawn are quite common now.

I've still to be convinced that upholstered outdoor furniture can be a worthwhile investment in the UK, particularly in the north and the Gulf-Stream blessed west. Our damp and rainy climate will mean those plush cushions are only inviting and dry on a few days of the year, and surely algae and moulds will soon find them just as inviting. You can bet these microorganisms will be more dedicated than we are in their occupation of the garden furniture, sticking it out in conditions when we prefer to be indoors occupying a warm, dry sofa with the benefit of central heating. Ultimately, it'll be the little guys who win the custody battle and the outdoor seating will languish in a sorry state, in all but those gardens with the most diligent scrubbing and mould removal regimes. Even with the protection of a pergola, canopy or some form of pavilion-style roofing with zip-closing side 'walls', humid air and the occasional horizontal rain will mean padded furniture is always prone to mildew and other microorganisms that thrive in dampness.

Although the idea of very comfortable seating in the garden is appealing, for many of us, the climate really won't let us use outdoor furniture often enough to make the cost-per-use value worthwhile. It might make more sense to carry cushions and blankets from indoors to make ourselves more comfortable on benches and more traditional wood or metal seating, taking them indoors again at the end of each day.

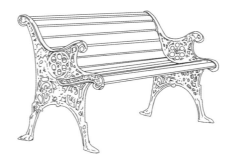

If, however, all this slightly sourpuss-toned reasoning has left your desire for garden sofas undampened (unlike the cushions left out in last night's downpour), let's consider how to avoid plastics. Many of the most common models on offer in the UK today are made from a woven plastic, mimicking the natural rattan of old-style wicker chairs. Wicker weave finishes are very attractive when new but provide a perfect habitat for moulds and algae, with so many little nooks and crannies throughout the weave and will therefore require an intensive maintenance and cleaning regime. Manufacturers claim they can be left out in all weathers, 365 days of the year. Perhaps this is true in warm dry climates but in the, ahem, changeable British weather, expect mould. The woven surface may also use up more plastic to manufacture than items with a smooth, solid finish.

Synthetic rattan used in this furniture is composed of strips of polyethylene (PE) plastic, or less commonly, polyurethane or PVC (polyvinylchloride). PE is recyclable, and this seems to be the basis for claims by retailers and manufacturers that it is 'eco-friendly' or easy on the environment in some way. They may have a point, to an extent: PE synthetic rattan will be durable and can be left outdoors year-round, cleaning regime notwithstanding, so it may outlast many alternative materials. And, in the tradition of so many environmental questions, the original natural rattan fibre, derived from palm trees, is not without its detrimental effects on ecosystems. With rising demand for rattan products, many of the harvested species are threatened with extinction, and unsustainable extraction methods can cause forest degradation and loss of biodiversity. Processing rattan to make the fibres ready for weaving often involves chemicals that pollute land and water and threaten the health of the workers and nearby communities. But where would you take your PE rattan sofa for 'recycling'? I have only ever seen them in the landfill skip at the local recycling depot. Being made of mixed materials (often a metal frame underneath the rattan weave), they are not a straightforward prospect for recycling.

Perhaps the simplest alternative, then, is a wooden (or metal) sofa with removable weatherproof cushions. Garden centres and some larger home décor stores sell several models of this type of garden sofa, but the padding element is often a complicating factor for anyone seeking to avoid plastic. This probably applies to many of the upholstered garden furniture products on sale. Outdoor, waterproof cushions are generally made with polyester and acrylic covers to make them waterproof, synthetic fibres that don't biodegrade at all quickly and will probably shed microfibres when washed. The fillings are typically a combination of polyurethane foam, polypropylene and polyester wadding, all synthetic, plastic-based materials. In short, these are not a plastic-free way to go. It might be best to bring cushions from indoors on dry days. Or investigate cushions with non-synthetic waddings in covers made from oilcloth (fabric treated with boiled linseed oil or similar oil-based coverings to waterproof it) or waxed fabrics, which are usually treated with beeswax or sometimes soya or paraffin wax to make them waterproof. To prolong the life of cushions, bring them under cover when rain is forecast, air them well on sunny days and store them, as far as possible, out of the damp.

As an aside, solid wooden benches and chairs not only look great and last for years but make the most comfortable and safe choice for older people or gardeners with certain disabilities and health conditions. They offer strong arms on which to support yourself when sitting or pushing yourself up to standing. The wood will tend to dry quickly after rain and feel warmer than metal seating, so is often the most comfortable option. Well-crafted wooden benches have curves in all the right places and rounded edges on every slat, making them so comfortable that cushions are often not required.

GARDEN LIGHTS

There's an overwhelming range of garden lighting options, including lots of solar powered ones. As with many other products, cheaper will tend to mean mass-produced and lots of not-so-durable, lower quality plastic components. This is bad news for those of us striving to be plastic-free gardeners, but very often for our pockets too as cheaper lighting will malfunction or fall apart more quickly. This is especially true for solar lighting: the very cheap products are so often a false economy, failing within a few months, and made predominantly from throwaway plastics, mixed with other materials, often in tiny parts which really complicates any recycling effort. The garden lighting market is truly saturated with poorly made products that offer little prospect of being reused or recycled.

It may be useful before purchasing to give some thought to how much enjoyment you might get in return for your investment in garden lighting. In the UK, long summer evenings mean that solar or sensor-controlled lights won't come on until you've gone indoors after dark, and there may be few occasions on which it's warm enough to sit out after sunset and appreciate the lighting. As the nights draw in, and the temperature drops, we spend less time outdoors in the evenings. Even if you plan to admire the lighting from indoors, once darkness falls, the double glazing in most homes will reflect your own cosy indoor scene and the room lighting, mostly blotting out your view of the garden lights. Having said that, a thoughtfully underlit specimen tree or some twinkly lights along a decking bannister can be beautiful. Where possible, opt for lighting made from glass within metal frames and structures and pay a little more for good quality materials that will last. You can find garden lighting specialists online and that way you'll be able to read reviews of the relative quality of each product, and a little more detail about the materials used in their manufacture. A good garden centre should also be able to recommend the most durable and reliable lights.

For any lighting that is to be installed and linked to a power supply, always hire a qualified, reliable electrician. Stating the obvious perhaps, but hopefully this advice won't offend too many readers, given the sometimes over-enthusiastic tendency for some gardeners to take a have-a-go, DIY attitude beyond realistic limits. For the more adventurous, there are online tutorials for making your own solar panels from old radiators and other recycled materials.

One last thought: could you instead use candles in storm lanterns for your garden lighting requirements?

LANDSCAPING MATERIALS

In the world of hard landscaping, perhaps more than in any other area, the warnings about alternatives sometimes having few advantages over plastic-based materials may apply. Slabs made from Indian sandstone may have been mined under terrible working conditions and with damaging environmental effects too, while certain timbers used for decking and other garden structures could have been extracted using less than responsible forestry practices, despite deterrents such as the EU Timber Regulations. While it's generally good to question our reliance on plastics, too narrow a focus can lead to choices with environmental and social impacts that are equally damaging, and sometimes worse. The watchword is research, and careful comparison to be sure that what you are buying is, on balance, better than what you are rejecting.

A second reason for a slightly more nuanced approach to plastics in relation to landscaping relative to other sectors is that, in general, landscaping materials stay in place for decades, so are less disposable. The risk of waste littering the land or reaching the ocean is lower when things are discarded at a slower rate. The most common materials used for land-scaping include stone, timber, concrete slabs and plastic/resin bonded gravels. In the last couple of decades, we've seen new products on offer including plastic moulded to look like wood or stone, and composites made of timber/sawdust or ground-up stone blended with polymers. These materials are used for decking, modular planting boxes and raised contain-ers, benches, blocks for making walls and even 'cast' stone paving.

The sturdiness and weatherproof nature of these materials are highlighted as advantages, as well as their low maintenance requirements. Although we must consider whether these claims are as good as the marketing brochures say, if true they need to be factored into the equation. If you really can save several years' worth of decking oil in tins, cleaning fluids in plastic bottles, paint brushes and scrubbing brushes by installing plastic or composite decking in place of timber, these saved resources must be weighed against the impacts of plastic production and (eventual) disposal.

Despite the complexity of such questions, it can often be useful to do a simple cost-benefit analysis ahead of prospec-tive purchases, comparing the expected longevity of alterna-tive products. A thin pine bench costing £50 might need replacing five times during the lifespan of a thick hardwood bench so to make a true comparison, you may need to multiply the cost of the pine bench by five. While based mainly on cost and durability, this exercise also sheds some light on the environmental impact of comparable products by helping us focus on how long they may last before we dispose of them.

With landscaping more than many other areas, the decision on which material to use comes down to wider considerations than just plastic/plastic-free. If you do anticipate using particular materials for a long time, it may be acceptable to opt for some that are made of plastic or incorporate a little plastic or resin, if they will reduce your need to use paints, oils and plastic packaged rust-removing chemicals. It goes almost without saying that very cheap, thin plastic items, like the stepping-stones in the shape of sliced log sections seen in some outlets are less likely to endure many seasons of use and harsh weather and so will become a waste problem more rapidly. Another consideration is that larger, more expensive materials like decking boards or bench slats are more likely to be reused or recycled than just dumped or discarded.

ARTIFICIAL TURF

A divisive subject at the best of times, particularly among gardeners, artificial turf is having a bit of a resurgence, if the gardens of Perth and the aisles of Scottish garden centres are any kind of guide. Only the most grudging commentator would deny that artificial turf has improved by a country mile since its toy-town incarnations of a few decades ago. There are now products with a more naturalistic fibre mix and colour range that are a little more difficult to spot if laid well.

As with other artificial plant products, turf promises the

colour and look of a well-tended lawn without the maintenance burden of mowing, feeding and edging. In certain situations, it's clear why it might appeal. But for the purposes of
avoiding or reducing plastic use in the garden, it's not an
option that offers very much at all. Artificial turf is made from
polyethylene, a polymer and might very well outlast any
trees we may plant, looking green and freshly mown long
after you've hung up your gardening boots. The best alternative options depend on your reasons for considering artificial
turf. If low maintenance is the main aim, consider laying
paving or gravel (to a good depth so plastic membrane is not
needed) or a mix of the two. Bark or wood chippings are
another groundcover option, cheaper than gravel but they
will need replacing more often. If the green and fresh look of
a lawn appeals but mowing does not, consider making a herb
or wildflower lawn that doesn't need mowing very much,
except perhaps for cutting a swathe or path through the
middle. These can be planted from seed mixes or laid as
specialist turf and, as with conventional lawns, will provide
food and habitat for wildlife.

In some situations, perhaps for some of us who are not so
physically able as we once were, the installation of a plastic
lawn might take away the burden of mowing and allow us to
enjoy the garden more, to focus on other tasks. For many
people, a garden isn't a garden without a lawn, and if we
can't maintain a live lawn, artificial turf may be the way to go.
It is a question for each gardener in their own situation: the
desire for a low maintenance lawn may outrank the desire to
reduce plastic, and the costs of the various alternatives will
also inform the final decision.

In areas of the world where water shortages are a problem,
such as parts of Australia, the cultivation of lawns is seen as

wasteful. In these circumstances, the use of artificial turf could be a way for people to have the enjoyment of a lawn without wasting the precious resource of water. An even better option, perhaps, though I'm not sure how feasible, would be a drought tolerant species mix to create a kind of 'lawn' that doesn't require irrigation. Just as new herb and wildflower 'lawn' matrices are being developed in Europe, might it be possible to find a mix of low maintenance, drought tolerant, low growing plants that would cover an area of garden in low rainfall areas and serve some of the same functions as the beloved green lawn?

GROUND STABILISATION & PROTECTION SYSTEMS

Quite common now in places where car parking space is installed on turfed areas or to make grassy or gravel areas firm and stable for wheelchairs, prams, cars and mobility scooters, 'turf guard' landscaping tiles can now be found underneath many areas of public and private landscaping. These little cellular 'paving slabs' are in fact sturdy inter-locking plastic frames housing square or honeycombed grid centres into which soil and lawn seed or gravel may be set. The grids are quite a wonder product all round, except from the perspective of trying to reduce plastic use, as they're made from a sturdy, presumably long-lasting version of the menace material.

Happily, at least one UK company is offering an alternative model made from recycled plastic that goes some way at least to assuaging concerns about overuse of virgin plastics. Eco Grid is made in Germany from 100% recycled MDPE and various suppliers in the UK sell it both retail and wholesale.

The grids seem to come with a 20-year guarantee from some stockists which gives further reassurance of their lasting, non-disposable nature, and some hope that they won't be contributing to marine pollution, at least in the short to medium term.

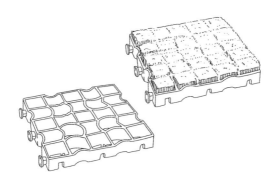

As ever, if you're considering installing one of these grid systems, go back to the root of your decision-making process and consider what it is you're trying to achieve. If you're just trying to create a stable surface for footpaths, you may be able to achieve that with paths built from a hardcore or 'road metal' base and compacted fine grit, e.g. 'whin dust' or quarry dust on top. Edging could be made from wood battens or steel edging products such as 'Everedge'. The same materials could be used for car parking areas, and indeed are found at many Forestry Commission sites. Wooden board-walk type paths may also be suitable, depending on the location and what you want to achieve.

As an aside, if you are installing ground stabilisation grid systems, read a little about Sustainable Urban Drainage Systems (SUDS) and think about how water infiltration might affect your new landscape surface. Drainage is important to consider – whichever landscaping materials you're using. Simple modifications, such as leaving a small space between tiles (some systems allow for this, others 'lock' tiles together) can make all the difference to ensuring good water management in your garden.

Avoid	Try
Plastic, upholstered outdoor furniture.	Wood or metal furniture, padded with cushions brought from indoors.
Plastic landscaping materials that are thin, overly cheap or seem unlikely to last.	Paths of compacted hardcore and quarry dust. Board or timber walkways.

7

COMPOST AND SOIL FOOD

Soil is the nerve centre of your garden, the living foundation for everything else, with its own frenetic secret life going on just beneath the visible surface. Caring for your soil is possibly the most important thing you can do to improve your garden and you might think this would be one area where it's relatively simple to avoid plastics. After all, what are you going to do except help nature go about its business? Well, happily it is one of the easier areas in which to reduce plastic use, but even the vigilant can still be caught out. As we've seen, compost and soil improver, mulches, stone, grit and fertilizer are all typically sold in bags of heavy-duty plastic, and if you don't have room to make your own compost you may have no choice but to buy these, plastic and all. Even if you are a keen home composter, most people don't produce enough to cover all their garden potting and mulching needs. In spite of these circumstances, there are some ways to cut your plastic use down and to reuse or recycle.

BULK ORDERS

If you can, order larger amounts of soil conditioners, fertilizers and mulches like horse manure, compost, bark chippings etc. This will reduce the amount of plastic packaging used. Many suppliers will deliver compost and similar products loose or in a reusable 'tonne' bag, ideal if you have the space to receive a bulk delivery. Join forces with fellow gardeners, members of your gardening group or local allotmenteers to share a bulk order if you can't use it all on your own plot. Those with the biggest gardens could perhaps find a space to store the delivery until everyone is able to organise collection. As a fringe benefit to reducing plastic use, larger orders will generally also mean cost savings for everyone.

Alternatively, if you can find a local supplier, a friendly stable owner or farmer perhaps, go to pick up manure, bark mulch or top soil in a well-lined car boot or with a friend who has a trailer, or with your (zinc) buckets in the back of your car/bicycle panniers.

REUSE

The plastic sacks in which compost and manure are sold at garden centres can be repurposed as potato-growing sacks or for collecting leaves in to make leaf mould. Ideally, they should be black on the inside to help block light from developing roots and potato tubers and to create ideal conditions for the communities of microorganisms that turn leaves into leaf mould. Drainage holes punched in the bottom and sides are essential for water and air circulation, and the sacks can be rolled down from the top until they are the right height for whatever you're storing or planting.

Some gardeners use compost sacks for lining the car boot during garden centre visits or covering a patio or deck area that you want to protect from mess when potting on large containers.

MAKE YOUR OWN COMPOST

Making your own will reduce the need to buy (at least some of) your compost supply, which invariably comes in non-recy-clable plastic bags. Most home composting bins are made from plastic, but you can build your own or buy wooden models. There could be a lot more home composting going on if it weren't for certain misconceptions about the process, chief among them being the idea that it will attract rats. The most likely things to attract rats into gardens are not home compost bins, but rather seed falling from bird feeders, dropped scraps of cat and dog food, and pet faeces. Composting is a great way to recycle your food and garden waste, make a wonderful, free soil conditioner and save plastic.

TRADITIONAL COMPOST BAYS

Build New Zealand style compost bins from scrap wood: dimensions and instructions are available online, although you can adapt the measurements to fit your space. Essentially the aim is to build a three-sided bay with strong corner posts joined by horizontal planks. These don't have to be exactly lined up as a few gaps will allow air to circulate. At the front, ideally add two extra upright posts forming a narrow vertical channel to allow planks of the fourth, front wall to be slotted in and removed, giving access to turn or take out the compost. Often people build compost bins from used pallets, which can still be found if you ask around or via selling or 'pass it on' sites like Gumtree. You can use the pallets whole, just propping them up vertically and fixing to posts, or dismantle them and use the planks for a customized design.

Leaf Composting

Use jute hessian sacks to store your leaves in while they break down or make a leaf compost corral from chicken wire and posts. Leaf mould makes a fantastic seed compost or a great addition to any home potting compost recipe. It's also a good mulch to use around plants that like woodland conditions or slightly acid soil such as camelias and blueberries. Leaves will take around two years to rot down and need a little moisture and air circulation to allow the microbes to do their work. If you have lots of leaf litter it could be worth your while to build a dedicated leaf composting bay (perhaps an addition to an existing compost area, or a stand-alone bin in a quiet/hidden corner of the garden) from board or wire and posts.

Hessian sacks are a great option if you don't have the space for a whole bin or bay. Other gardeners put leaves into surplus plastic(!) compost bags with holes punched in the bottom. For all but the plastic-free purists, this is a practical option that uses existing plastic for a second time (and possibly more, reusing until the bags are no longer intact). At home, I use a spare wheelie bin that was left at the property by previous owners, with aeration holes drilled in the sides around the bottom 12 to 18 inches.

Other Methods

The Cone or Dalek Composter

The most commonly seen composting method in the UK is a plastic cone-shaped bin with a removable lid for adding in raw materials and a hatch in the bottom for taking out compost. These were given to householders free or at low prices under local authority schemes during the 1990s and the noughties. They are also sold very cheaply online and in garden centres and are easy to use and find space for. Of course, they're made from a big hunk of plastic, although they can in theory be recycled by companies that accept rigid plastics. The main hurdle, as so often, is in getting the compost bin into such reprocessing loops run by companies who typically deal only with large contractors.

For the home gardener, the best advice may be to keep on using your plastic cone composting bin(s) if you already have one, whether bought, received from the local authority or inherited. They do seem to be quite long lasting with the exception of some substandard early models that were prone to warping so that their lids wouldn't fit.

For those who don't have any composting facility in their garden but would like to start, consider the options here and weigh up your available space and kitchen and garden waste, along with the plastic involved in each method.

Green Johanna

Made of plastic but sturdy, long lasting and claiming to be 'rat proof' and with some other adaptations so you can safely compost meat and fish waste, cooked food and even chicken carcasses. This system is a hot composter and you can buy 'jackets' for winter to increase its insulation. The walls are made of quite thick plastic, so it's an investment in more plastic, but it looks very sturdy so you would expect it to last for many years.

The Traditional 'Heap'

Just pile up your compost materials in layers in a neat-ish stack. No bin or structure is used. Cover with an old carpet or other reusable textile to protect from heavy rain. This style can be messy-looking and some gardeners feel you lose some of the heating effect by not having walls to contain the compost and all its biological activity. But it won't cost you a penny and can be organised in a heartbeat. And of course, it's entirely free of plastic.

'Tumbler' Systems

These composters claim to make it easier to turn compost and promise faster results. Some rotate on an axel, others on a base, while yet others are rolled along the ground by human propulsion (i.e. you). They tend to be made of thick plastic or metal. A *Which* study found that tumbler models were actually slower to produce compost than systems like the New Zealand box style outlined above. Another drawback is that tumblers are supposed to work best when filled up in one go, so they're not a good option if you want somewhere to regularly put small amounts of garden and food waste. You may need a different place to put that sort of compost. Also, worms are excluded (they'd die when the drum heated up and be unable to escape anyway), so this form of composting relies on bacteria and fungi to break down the plant matter.

Not everyone does turn their compost, whether with an old-fashioned pitchfork or a gadget with a crank handle, which shows it is possible to get compost without any tumbling effort. Worms do the turning for us in traditional compost heaps, albeit perhaps at a slower pace than some may like, even if we don't disturb or agitate the material at all. In other words, if you want to try this method and avoid plastic, you can probably find a tumbling compost maker that's made from metal or wood and have a go. I have heard gardeners say they find the tumbler crank handles very heavy to turn. Some people take out the compost once it's reached a rough stage of decomposition and make a heap on the ground which allows worms to come in and do their work.

Hot Composting Methods

HotBin is the most prominent brand on sale at the moment. A super-insulated type of composter that can reach temperatures of 60C and claims to make compost in 30–90 days. Made of ARPRO® Expanded Polypropylene also known as 'EPP', it has a thick layer of insulating material around the central core where the composting happens. EPP looks like polystyrene but is not. The makers say it's a specialist, very durable plastic and that no CFCs (Chlorofluorocarbons) or HCFCs (Hydrochlorofluorocarbons) are used during the manufacturing process, just steam and water. The HotBin website says EPP is not a 'single-use' plastic, is fully recyclable and can be made into new products. They say the whole bin design consists of just 4% raw material and 96% air and that it's therefore resource efficient. It's quite hard to evaluate the resource efficiency since we don't really know the raw material to air ratio of other products and materials. Some prominent gardeners including our own Trellis patron, Jim McColl, MBE and garden writer Alys Fowler have endorsed the product and been impressed by the speediness of compost production. But it is clearly a new plastic product made from virgin plastic, and from that perspective, perhaps it wouldn't be the top choice for a plastic-free plot.

The Green Johanna mentioned above is also a hot composting bin. The permaculture people describe how to do hot composting without the need for an insulated bin. By using a normal metal bin or any vessel up to a maximum of one cubic metre, adding a nice balance of green and brown composting material, chopping your ingredients very small and turning regularly after the first few days, keeping the mix irrigated to the humidity of 'a wrung-out sponge', and covering with a tarpaulin, they say your compost can be ready in 18 days and can reach temperatures of 55–65C, killing pathogens and weed seed.

This can seem a bit laborious and perhaps illustrates why Hot Bin type composters are so appealing – though they do come with their manufacturer's stipulations about how much of each type of material and how small the pieces must be chopped before adding. They also cost more than the average compost bin at around £199 each.

When considering the pros and cons of hot composting, you might decide to opt for a compromise. By just giving a little more attention to the layering and chopping of material going into your compost heap, you might be able to speed things up. Meanwhile by cultivating a patient attitude, you can test the adage that good things come to those who wait.

Beehive Style

These wooden composters are built to look like beehives. To many this is a more attractive style of composter, and plastic-free, if more expensive than some models. The main difference is in the aesthetics and the plastic-free construction. The composting method and speed is likely to be similar to the plastic cone or New Zealand Box methods that many of us use at home.

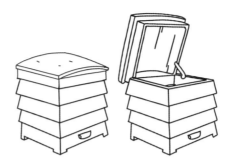

In-ground or Hole Composting

Essentially, you dig a hole and put kitchen scraps in, cover the hole when it's full up and move on to another area. Repeat. It's hard to see how you can beat this system for plastic-free credentials or economy, although it has some limitations in its productive effects. The nutrient enrichment of the soil will clearly be localised, and you don't have a product to scoop out and use where you most need it. Some gardeners dig a composting hole in a place where they plan to plant a tree, perhaps after a few months to allow the food waste to break down. Many people use a similar method to prepare a trench for growing beans, layering in food scraps in the weeks before they plant the bean seeds. The other disadvantage is the regular digging, which may not be for everyone.

WORM BIN COMPOSTING

Wormeries allow you to make solid worm compost and a liquid fertilizer from your kitchen food scraps. Many of the best-known worm bins are made mostly from plastic but there are lots of wooden models too, as well as plans available online for making your own wooden wormery.

BOKASHI

Based on a grain product (bran) inoculated with a mix of yeasts and bacteria that supercharges the decomposition process, Bokashi composting is a fermenting process that can cope with cooked foods including meat and other animal products. The action of the Bokashi culture happens in an anaerobic environment, as the material is packed down firmly and another bran layer spread on top. Many of the bins sold for this composting style are plastic but there are also stainless steel vessels on offer from Bokashi Direct (UK) and I feel sure that if you could carefully drill a hole to insert a tap (necessary to run off the liquid produced by fermentation) in a ceramic compost caddy, you could easily keep your bokashi in that. The resulting liquor is quite acidic and must be carefully diluted before use.

Avoid	Try
Plastic compost bins that look like they may be too small for your needs or too flimsy to last for long.	Bins made from spare timber or old pallets or from posts and chicken wire.
High-tech plastic composters making big claims.	Improving your existing compost setup by chopping raw materials smaller and layering with attention to moisture content and the balance of green and brown materials.
Plastic compost caddies or worm bins.	Zinc bucket, ceramic caddies (a repurposed biscuit jar, maybe?) and wooden worm bins.

8

SOCIAL EVENTS, FEASTS & CELEBRATIONS

Don't worry, I'm not here to rain on your garden festivities. Every now and then, a garden may be host to a gathering that requires food and drink to be served, plates and salads to be washed, seats to be set out and tables to be laid. Whether you're having a barbeque with your group to celebrate the harvest, the completion of a building project, or just inviting friends round for an al fresco tea and cakes moment, there are lots of plastic things begging to be taken home for just such an occasion. They will appeal to your desire for convenience, for a bargain, for shiny, colourful new things with the promise of brightening up your plot. Just a little forward planning and lateral thinking is all it takes to resist the allure of the great host of plastic picnicware, food wrapping, table decorations and tuck boxes.

Many in the food industry would argue that plastic packaging increases the shelf life of food products and reduces waste, improving hygiene and making transport more efficient. These are fair points and so here, as with every other aspect of plastic-free gardening, the picture is complicated. Food producers and retailers, however, are trying to reduce plastic waste and improve recycling rates (although it may always not seem that way to customers) so in this area as with so many others, the picture is constantly changing. Meanwhile, what follows is a little food for thought for those of us trying to reduce our use of plastic on an individual scale at garden feasts and social events. There are so many great alternatives now on offer, with many as convenient, bright, lightweight and affordable as their plastic counterparts.

PLATES AND CROCKERY

Cheap and cheerful plastic plates are sold, especially in picnic season, in many of our supermarkets, homeware and garden shops. The good news is that enamelled tin is an affordable alternative: light, portable, durable and almost unbreakable. Some bamboo and other plant fibre plates are now available too for parties or other events where disposable or low-frequency-use crockery is required. Sugarcane bagasse, wheat straw and banana leaves are just some of the plant materials now being made into compostable or biodegradable plates. The market is changing rapidly so the best advice is to search for what's available in your area to suit your budget and requirements. But beware, paper plates may often be coated in a thin layer of plastic which can make them a recycling impossibility, and none too useful for the compost heap either. Clearly, single-use plastic or polystyrene plates and bowls should be avoided where possible as they'll be very tricky to recycle and non-compostable, so exacerbating our plastic problem.

CUPS

There are many plastic and polystyrene cups on offer, marketed as convenient and often very cheap. Paper cups too are there on the shelves, but as with plates, many cups are coated with a fine plastic layer which makes it complicated, and probably not viable, to recycle them. The coffee shops in your town or village may well serve coffee in these single-use cups. Governments and retailers are waking up to the problems of single-use cups now and alternatives are beginning to crop up everywhere. Legislative changes are in the pipeline which will soon bring financial incentives to take your own cup to coffee shops and dodge the single-use, plastic-lined ones. Some cafes are already operating schemes like these and the trend looks set to increase as more responsibility is put upon retailers to deal with the waste their business generates and to recycle more.

Meanwhile, for situations that still seem to call for disposable cups, there are now compostable options, made from paper with a plant-starch inner coating that will biodegrade and allow recycling in some facilities. Vegware is perhaps the best-known brand in the UK, but for social gatherings at the Trellis Potting Shed, we also like Enviropack cups from Sarah's Coffee Company in Nuneaton. Many people are also investing in a 'cup for life' or 'Keep Cups', longer lasting vessels, often made of bamboo or glass and silicone, for you or your barista to fill daily. There are reviews of these popping up online, so you can figure out which brands and designs offer the most reliably sealed lids and will not taint the flavour of your *cortado*. But for your garden party hamper, you can also use ceramic or enamelled tin cups and traditional glasses. The inconvenient part is that there will be some washing up to do of course, but that's one for each of us to weigh up in a cost-benefit analysis on our personal ethics calculator.

In the UK, some summer festivals (even huge events like Glastonbury) have begun to ban sales of drinks in plastic cups and bottles, advising visitors to bring their own water bottles, and providing water standpipes instead.

CUTLERY

Bamboo or Vegware compostable cutlery is widely available now if you really need a disposable option. Bring your own metal cutlery from home or make portable finger food that requires no cutlery. Wraps, filled rolls, samosas, falafel, pies or slices of egg tortilla or quiche are some good examples that, with only a square of greaseproof paper, a cocktail stick perhaps, some kitchen paper or a napkin, will make the perfect party or picnic food, no cutlery required.

FOOD AND DRINK

As you'll be using up your own proud harvest, perhaps very little of what you serve at your garden gathering will come swaddled in plastic. Cordials made from the berry harvest could be served from glass bottles and jugs. If you've not managed Good Life levels of self-sufficiency, consider which items on your shopping list are most likely to be packaged in plastic and where you can find alternatives to these that will minimise packaging. Can you trade produce with other gardeners nearby? Are there greengrocers and dry goods shops in your town that still sell things loose or in paper bags? Can you ask guests to bake and bring something?

Drinks products are often some of the worst offenders in the plastic packaging rogues' gallery. Mineral water and carbonated soft drinks are typically sold in plastic bottles and often also shrink-wrapped inside another layer of plastic sleeve just for good measure. The caps of these bottles are often not recyclable or composed of a different plastic from the bottle itself which reduces the chances they will be successfully recycled through the right waste stream. Often, these drinks bottles are made of coloured plastic, which further complicates the recycling possibilities.

You can buy a gadget that pumps carbon dioxide gas into water to make fizzy drinks at home. This will reduce the need for buying single-use soft drink bottles. As an alternative, you could serve fruit punches, infusions and herb teas made from garden produce. Many fruit juices are sold in plastic-coated cardboard (sometimes Tetrapak) cartons which are not straightforward to recycle, requiring specialist equipment to separate the metal from the plastic and paper content. Not every local authority will necessarily have access to these. The

Tetrapak website carries information on which parts of the UK have such recycling plants, organised by local authority area. Try squeezing your own juice if you want to avoid purchasing beverages in packaging with plastic coating or find fruit juice in glass bottles that can be widely recycled.

Coffee and tea producers can be some of the worst plastic addicts, but increasingly there are plastic-free alternatives. Coffee can be bought in bean form or freshly ground in paper packets, tea is another product that was once only sold loose leaf and now can be found in that form again, often from specialist shops. If you are buying tea bags, try to recognise, and avoid, the brands that individually wrap each teabag in plastic envelopes or vacuum pack tea bags in non-recyclable plastic film inside the box, and those who make their tea bags from little pyramids of plastic net. Other manufacturers add in a little plastic to the tea bag material itself for good measure, even though it looks to all intents and purposes like paper. This is hard to believe when you see the tea bags: they do look so papery. However, a year or two later, when you find yourself picking out little shrivelled white tea bag shrouds from your compost, it becomes very much more believable that there was something more environmentally persistent in the mix.

Following protests, some brands including Co-op, PG Tips and Clipper are phasing out all plastic components in their tea bags. Pukka tea is also plastic-free and some ranges from Aldi and Waitrose are without plastic. If you are using loose tea, you'll need an infuser or tea strainer, usually made from stainless steel, sometimes bamboo, and a teapot, of course: enamelware, ceramic, porcelain, or glass, take your pick. With teapots, happily, there's lots of choice and a plastic one wouldn't be much use anyway. All you need worry about is trying to find one that's a good pourer.

Even coffee capsules for espresso machines are available in compostable materials now (e.g. Dualit), although don't be surprised if the compostable pods and boxes come wrapped in a fair quantity of plastic. Another point to note is that many of these coffee pods are not likely to break down in garden compost and will need to be put into a bin that gives them a chance of ending up in an industrial composting system.

Many of us will have no idea what this means in relation to which kerbside recycling bin to put them in, nor whether our local authority has access to such an industrial composting facility, so here once again, the cycle is far from clear or well thought out. But it's good to know that at least there are ways to make our favourite national drinks without putting even more persistent plastics into the environment.

Milk can still be found in glass bottles in some places – usually via a delivery service or a farm shop. For everyone else, the Tetrapak carton or plastic milk bottle seems all but unavoidable if you want to serve milk to go with your tea or coffee. The usual suggestions of reducing plastic packaging waste by buying in larger quantities don't work so well for a product so perishable as milk. The only thing I can advise here is to cultivate a taste for black tea or coffee, or switch to herbal tea.

While a return to milk in glass bottles may appeal to the nostalgic among us, some analysts have argued that Tetrapak cartons actually cause fewer emissions in their manufacture than do glass bottles. This doesn't help much with the disposal problem, though. The litre-sized cartons used to contain so many drinks products are made from aluminium and plastic bonded to card with a plastic screw top, which is why specialist equipment and processes are required to separate the layers ahead of recycling them. They are, however, widely recycled, in the UK at least. Check the Tetrapak website map to establish that there are appropriate recycling facilities in your area. If your council accepts these cartons in your recycling bins, you can be pretty sure they have a recycling facility within striking distance.

Supermarkets are starting to wake up to consumer demand for reduced plastic packaging but it's a slow process and if you want to help speed it up, make your feelings known to retailers. As with all these emerging products and market changes, if enough people join in, it might help accelerate the process of reaching a tipping point.

TRANSPORTING AND STORING FOOD AND LEFTOVERS

Consider using beeswax food wrappers instead of cling film or zip-lock sandwich bags. These are squares of cotton coated with beeswax or soya wax that you lay over the top of a casserole or salad dish or cake container, pressing the wrap against the edges to create a seal. The wax makes them stick to the rim of the dish. Beeswax covers can also be wrapped around sandwiches or slices of pie and wedges of cheese, in the same way as you might wrap food with cling film. Just rinse them with water after each use, dry thoroughly and they can be reused for around a year. They come in various sizes and I can testify to their effectiveness and ease of use. You can buy beeswax wrappers or even make your own, following instructions on various websites. As far as I can grasp, this involves sprinkling grated or pelleted beeswax onto squares of fabric and gently warming them in a low oven to melt the wax, then brushing it into an even layer over the fabric.

Use glass casserole and freezer dishes with silicone lids or steel tiffin tins to store and transport food. Tupperware, the traditional classic, is plastic of course, but since many households have a stash of these famous food storage tubs, it wouldn't make sense to turf them all out into landfill. Often, they've been in use for decades, which lifts them out of the zone of single- or short-term use plastics, and perhaps makes them a justifiable part of the food storage and transport arsenal.

WASHING UP

Products like washing-up liquid and hand soap tend to come in plastic bottles and in the case of hand soap, with a plastic pump mechanism inside to help you extract every last drop. While some brands offer a refill service via local shops, many of us are not near one of those refill stations and many more lack the organisational rigour required to remember to pack the empty bottle before heading out to do the shopping. You can buy glass, steel or ceramic bottles for pumping soap, and decant into these from a large, catering-sized container; this reduces, rather than eliminates, your plastic use.

Alternatively, find recipes online for grating bar soap into water to make liquid soap. From personal experience and the anecdotes of friends, I can tell you this may be time consuming and yield variable results. You could wash dishes with soap flakes, sold in cardboard boxes, like Granny used to do (just dissolve a spoonful in water in the washing-up bowl. Add some lemon juice or lavender oil to scent it and cut through grease).

A slightly more *alternative* alternative is to use 'Soap Nuts', fruit of an Indian Tree, Sapindus mukorossi (also called Soap Berries or Indian Soap Fruits). These can be put a few at a time in a cotton pouch or a sock and, once in water, will release their saponins (soap-like compounds) and create a dirt-busting, silky, slightly foamy emulsion that will gently but effectively clean your dishes (and hands, and clothes). They can be reused and later composted. Soap Nuts are also used for laundering clothes so could replace plastic laundry detergent bottles too. Instead of a plastic washing-up basin, you could use an enamel-plated metal one, or just keep the sink very clean and wash dishes directly in that.

MICROBEADS

Microbeads, those totally unnecessary little plastic particles in some soaps and cosmetic creams, rose swiftly to public prominence in recent years and a change in legislation was seen soon after. But while the ban came into force in January 2018 and some retailers already resolved via their own policies not to sell microbead products, you may still be unpleasantly surprised by old stock sitting on the shelves and only discover the offending grainy particles when you get home. Some grainy ingredients in cosmetic products may be made of nuts or other biodegradable materials, so it's worth checking the label if unsure.

Do let retailers know, and indeed the regulator, the environment department of the local council, if you think a company is flouting the law. Additionally, you can find out more about how to avoid microbeads at the Ban the Bead website and social media channel. The ban only applies to cosmetics – some industrial cleaning products continue to include microbeads, as highlighted by a recent report on microbeads in the North Sea outlining how these plastic beads enter the sea as a waste product of the oil industry.

Avoid	Try
Plastic plates, cups, and cutlery especially single-use, 'disposable' products.	Enamelled tin picnicware, bamboo and plant starch cutlery such as Vegware and compostable cups.
Food and drink products wrapped in (excessive) plastic packaging.	Buying produce loose from greengrocers and shops that sell in bulk or by weight and offer paper or other recyclable/compostable packaging.

9

CLOTHING

Gardeners often are regarded as people who don't think a lot about the clothes they wear, so absorbed in the flora and fauna in our little square of paradise we've no time for superficial concerns like appearances and matters sartorial. That's probably an outdated idea. Modern gardeners need to be comfortable and protected in the garden and while the horticultural world may not on the whole be renowned for interest in dress and outward appearances, they do like to feel good in their clothes. What's more, a lot of gardening is concerned with creating and enhancing beauty, so honing our skills does involve an increasing discernment in matters of design and aesthetics. These sensibilities don't confine themselves to the chlorophyll-coloured segments of the world. Once attuned, we start to notice good and bad design and things that enhance or detract in every sphere of life.

Arguably, the need to feel so at ease in our clothes that we can become entirely absorbed by gardening, demands a higher than usual level of comfort and functionality. Leaky waterproofs or scratchy uncomfortable clothing is a constant irritation and distraction and therefore unlikely to earn a place for long in most garden wardrobes. When you stop to think about the stringent considerations of wear and tear that gardening clothes are subjected to, the list of demands we make of clothes begins to look exacting indeed.

Gardeners are likely to be out in all weathers, exposed to sharp implements and compost, soil, rank-smelling liquid fertilizers, dusty doses of lime, plant sap and pigmented pollen among other substances that can easily damage and wear out the finish of fabrics. We need to be protected from the tools we're using, from thorns and stinging plants and insects, from plants that can mark the skin and cause allergic reactions, and perhaps from scratchy grasses and branches and so on. The choice of fabrics that are up to these tasks, while still feeling comfortable against the skin, is rather limited. At the same time, we may want to have our hands and sometimes our limbs free to be able to feel the plants that we're working with, to enjoy the sun's warmth and the fresh air on our skin and yet to be protected from sun and wind burn, or from midge bites. This means that, far from throwing on any old clothes, decisions about what we wear in the garden may be even more stringent than for some formal wear.

WARM AND FLEECY LAYERS

The first item we need to consider is a bit of a phenomenon. Many of us have begun to wear this garment like a second skin. It's the fleece, the ubiquitous zip-up or pullover garment, modern usurper of the woolly jumper in many wardrobes. Incredibly common now on a global scale, it's hard to believe Polar Fleece fabric didn't exist until 1979, expressly designed to substitute, or improve on, wool garments. Many people think of fleeces as being super gentle on the environment, something that is in no small part thanks to the marketing put about by fleece retailing companies. It is a fact that many fleece clothes are sold as environmentally friendly products, being made from recycled plastic drinks bottles. While making use of a waste product is a good start – recycling plastic bottles at least means they're not going to landfill – it doesn't get away from the fact: fleece fabric is a plastic textile. Lots of fleece is not made from recycled plastic drinks bottles but instead is virgin polymer from raw materials. So, many fleeces on the market and in our wardrobes are just another plastic product, subject to the same problems of disposal after their useful life is done. Fleece clothing won't degrade and will be hanging around in landfill or swimming in our seas for centuries.

Beyond this, the microfibre fleece has some other, less than glowing environmental quirks and that may come as bad news given how attached we've become to these warm, cheap, convenient garments. Apart from being essentially a plastic- or petroleum-derived product in the same way as plastic plant pots, recent research suggests that fleece fabrics release many tiny fragments every time they are laundered, and these go into the water system, into water courses and eventually to the sea. There, they can be absorbed into the food chain, where they can affect wildlife and ecosystems in ways we don't yet understand, but which many expect will be negative.

Synthetic microfibres have been found in abundance on shores near waste-water outlets, and scientists have found them apparently tangled into the intestines of fish. One of the many worries about tiny particles of plastic is that they may accumulate as they move up the food chain. They're small enough to get into the bodies of tiny organisms near the bottom of the food chain. As these small creatures are consumed by their predators, say shrimp and snails, and they in turn are consumed by fish and larger animals, it's possible that the levels of microplastics in the bodies of animals further up the chain are getting progressively more concentrated. To make things worse, microfibres seem to be very good at absorbing organic pollutants which they then carry into the bodies of the creatures who swallow them, where they too can become concentrated, potentially to toxic levels.

Essentially, our fleece use means we are still putting more plastic into the environment, and the microfibres they shed may be as bad or more of a threat to the environment than discarded plastic bottles before they were recycled into fleece. That's probably a bit of a blow to lots of us because they seemed to be a great modern convenience in every other way: warm, lightweight and practical; easy to wash and care for. Fleece clothes are soft, cosy and comfortable and come in a huge variety of colours and styles.

Until better options are found, however, perhaps we should dial down our enthusiasm for microfibre textiles and return to some of the more traditional alternatives. We could rediscover the old staples such as woolly jumpers and waxed cotton jackets that both have decent waterproofing and insulating properties. Classics like wool, gaberdine, quilted jackets, flannel or wool shirts, and thermal base-layers (silk or merino wool) under moleskin or corduroy, will ensure you're well protected in the colder months or the unexpected downpours of summer. Wool socks, hats and gloves are comfortable to wear, warm and breathable. A waterproofing layer can be added by wearing latex gloves (or latex-coated cotton) over a woollen pair. Cotton drill or twill, linen, bamboo fibre, silk, wool, hemp and other plant and animal derived fabrics will be your best bets for the warmer months, breathable, soft and lightweight as well as biodegradable. Straw or canvas hats are a good bet for keeping the sun off your head.

One small product may help reduce the microfibre shedding of fleece fabrics into the seas. The recently developed Cora Ball claims to capture around 30% of the microfibres coming out of your laundry in the washing machine and stop them from flowing into public waterways. The Guppyfriend wash bag promises to do a similar thing in a slightly different way, by enclosing your microfibre clothes in a special textile membrane that won't let the fibres escape. Presumably other good ideas like these are in the prototype or trial phases: keep a look out for news and reviews. Perhaps there will soon be other ways to reduce the impact of our cosy layers.

DAISY ROOTS & OTHER FOOTWEAR

Wellington boots, the eternal staple by the back door, can be a sustainable choice. Latex rubber will break down over time, although it will take quite a lot longer than you might think, certainly longer than manufacturers sometimes claim. The last few years have seen a few cousins of the original knee-length Wellington boot come to market, shorter boots at calf length, 'wellibobs' (ankle-height boots) and rubber garden clogs. All of these are generally made from rubber harvested from trees in Brazil, and transformed via the famous Vulcanisation process, but some may be synthetic rubber. Both synthetic and naturally derived rubber can be degraded by bacteria that occur in the soil, although they may need some help from biotechnology to ensure they are exposed to the right bacteria at the right time to speed up degradation.

Beware PVC wellies, however, which are becoming more and more common and apart from being plastic, may also be less comfortable with less 'give' in them than rubber boots. If welly boots are very glossy or transparent, they may well be made from PVC.

Leather or canvas boots can be fantastic in the garden and many gardeners have a favourite old faithful pair that has served them for many years. A good pair of leather boots with a steel toecap should see you through decades if well cared for with regular application of a waterproofing polish. Here, as so often, there's no easy way to choose between the alternatives: the environmental costs of raising animals then tanning their skins to make leather boots must be balanced against any plastic savings.

Some boots contain a reinforced sole and toe cap that are made from TPU (thermoplastic polyurethane) or even aluminium. Kevlar (as used in bullet-proof vests and bike tyres) is also sometimes used, one of a number of specialist polymer-based materials valued for their strength and protective qualities. Kevlar is supposed to be five times as strong as steel. This is one of those areas where there are not very many alternatives and it may be hard to find out which material a manufacturer has used to line the toe cap of a boot. Given the importance of protecting your feet, the best route may be to try to get as many years of service from your boots as possible by taking good care of them, rather than agonising over their precise construction.

GORE-TEX

Many outdoor garments are made with Gore-Tex because it's waterproof, lightweight and said not to make you sweat. This fabric is another polymer – a synthetic textile of the plastics family and until 2013 depended for its manufacturing process on fluorosurfactant PFOA, a persistent environmental contaminant. Another chemical PFC, also a perfluorinated compound, has replaced PFOA in the process but some people have questioned whether it is much of an improvement. Now even PFCs are to be removed from the manufacturing process by 2020. The Gore-Tex company says that it's the durability of their clothing that makes them a more environmentally positive choice as, if they're worn for many years, they won't cause so much waste as garments that are discarded sooner. There don't seem to be any clear ways to recycle Gore-Tex garments, although the company says it is making efforts to include more recycled materials in the textiles it produces.

Another company that makes breathable waterproof clothing, SympaTex, says its textile membranes are 100% recyclable. They are made of polyester with polyether and are marketed under various fabric brand names.

Many other waterproof clothes are made from synthetic fabrics like nylon, acrylic and polyester. None of these will compost or breakdown quickly, though they may be recyclable in some cases. Overall, there's a risk that they will contribute to our legacy of waste that persists in the environment long after we're gone.

For those bamboozled by the textile technology, the most sustainable alternatives might be wool or waxed cotton jackets (the original 'oilskins' which were made from worn-out sail-cloth treated with boiled linseed oil) or perhaps leather. Modern 'oilskins' tend to be PVC or fabric coated with other plastics, so it pays to look behind the marketing language.

Some manufacturers produce waterproofing waxes with which to treat fabrics: Nik Wax is one example. Although it's easy to be dazzled by the chemistry, it seems that although some of these products are 'water-based' as opposed to solvent-based, they do use 'dispersal agents' such as poly-acrylates (essentially – you guessed it – polymers). My understanding of the relevant science is too limited to make much sense of this, but I assume the dispersal agents help distribute the waterproofing chemicals evenly over all the surfaces of the textiles in your coat or over-trousers. Whatever their role in the process, it's clear that plastics and polymers are used in the manufacture of one of the most common waterproofing products, so not the most obvious thing to add to the shopping list for gardeners striving to be plastic-free. Nik Wax is at least transparent about their ingredients, publishing lists of what goes into all their products, and does include some water-based components in the mix. That at least gives you the information you need to do a little research on the alternatives before making your choices.

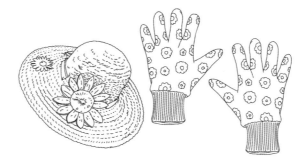

GLOVES

A warm pair of protective work gloves are essential – especially for tasks like clearing up rose or gooseberry prunings, and any outdoor jobs in winter. Leather gloves with a warm lining are a dependable choice although thorns can still poke through the leather and without a good waterproof finish they can let in the cold and wet. You may want to seek out a pair with extra layers of reinforcement to avoid being spiked.

Some gloves come with a steel mesh inner layer (sometimes also with Kevlar, the synthetic alternative material developed by DuPont) to help protect hands from injury. In the garment and fish-processing industries, pattern cutters and fish gutters wear steel mesh chainmail gloves to protect their hands from fast moving, demonically efficient blades. This might be an option to consider if your main priority with gloves is protection from thorn scratches and cuts. Steel mesh gloves are available online at reasonable prices and are mostly plastic-free. It may seem like overkill for gardeners, but after you've pruned the gooseberry bushes for another year, things may look very different.

You can also buy thick fabric gloves with a rubberised coating over the fingers and palm to provide some winter waterproofing, often with thermal linings too. These are well worth seeking out; the latex will degrade over time and not persist in the environment. They're my go-to gloves for year-round use (mine are from Briers) and they do give some protection from thorns. Keep a few pairs of gloves on rotation so you always have a warm, dry pair ready to use. Here again, gloves offered as being waterproof might come with a plastic coating, so try to research the product before buying.

SUNGLASSES

Some brands will tend to use glass lenses and metal arms, but the vast majority of sunglasses now use plastic frames and, in many cases, plastic lenses too. The component materials change every season for most brands, and personal requirements for lens type and preference for frame shapes is so idiosyncratic that it's probably impossible to offer much advice here. Optical plastics like Trivex are now such lightweight, shatterproof and finely tuned materials that they are often considered superior to glass. When the best option for your comfort, safety and eye health is a plastic, it makes it much harder to justify seeking out a glass alternative. Here again, sunglass lenses are hardly a disposable product, and so may not be a priority area in which to switch away from plastic.

Higher quality brands will be better for your eye health in general, so perhaps the main focus should be on seeking out something well-made that will last. As with all more considered purchases, time spent doing some research into the materials among all the other considerations about UVA and UVB protection, how well the frame fits your face and the colour and glare cutting properties of the lenses will repay itself. An optician should be able to advise which materials are in a given pair of sunglasses. It goes without saying that looking after your shades carefully will extend their life and postpone the date of their reuse or recycling, notwithstanding changes to optical prescriptions.

Avoid	Try
Microfibre fleece.	Woollen jumpers, waxed cotton jackets, corduroy, moleskin, canvas/twill or heavy denim.
Plastic welly boots.	Rubber boots, leather or canvas boots.
Plastic-coated gloves.	Rubber coated gloves, leather with waterproof wax applied.

10

WHAT TO DO WITH THE PLASTIC YOU HAVE?

Realism has been one of the guiding maxims of this guide, albeit realism tempered with a large dose of optimism about the potential for the small-scale actions of gardeners to add up, collectively, to a sizeable positive difference. The reality, for most of us, is that we have far more plastic in our gardening lives presently, than we might like. Put that together with a lack of good, locally accessible recycling options and confusion over terminology and we have a stubborn and immediate problem. As more stories and images of plastic marine litter and afflicted wildlife appear in our print and online reading material, on podcasts, radio and TV it can start to create a strong emotional reaction against all things plastic. These sorts of doom-filled stories can fuel a communal hysteria that's not conducive to rational solutions. A piecemeal, emotionally driven approach runs the risk of being unsatisfying and ineffective, so how should we best tackle the problem of the plastic we already have?

Once you've invested your hard-earned money in things that happen to be made of plastic, it doesn't make much sense, financially or environmentally to rush to turf them all out, no matter how badly plastic's reputation is tainted. One of the most sensible things you can do is use plastic articles until the end of their useful life. While it might be nice to look out over your garden or survey your houseplant collection and know there's as little plastic as possible lurking among the green, it may be more sensible to adopt a gradualist approach rather than tipping everything out in a fever.

Companies such as TerraCycle, RECOUP, Impact Recycling and Filcris can recycle or find ways of repurposing unwanted plastics including rigid plastic as found in watering cans, garden furniture and play equipment such as sandpits. The reprocessed plastic can be used to create new products – possibly for the garden, but for other sectors too. The big problem is that these companies mainly deal with other larger businesses and are not generally set up to be accessible to the humble domestic gardener. One of the reasons for this is that in order to run a viable recycling or reprocessing business, they need a certain minimum volume of incoming plastic materials. But the cost of having to staff receiving depots or send collecting vehicles out on circuitous routes to every person who had a recyclable item to pick up would be prohibitive. The most efficient way for them to work is to have other businesses collect plastics and deliver them to the reprocessing plant. The recycling infrastructure is just not quite what it could be yet, although things are changing. Where possible, seek out schemes that can receive rigid plastics, such as participating garden centres. It might also be wise to sound out suppliers before buying any plastic materials – for example, ask polytunnel companies if they will accept the old tunnel covers back when they're ready for recycling.

There will be many ways to approach your personal plastic-free nirvana, but I offer this methodical and simple path as a starting point. By taking a planned, gradualist line, there's a better chance of making change we can sustain. Reduce, reuse and recycle, in that order, is a useful rule of thumb.

1. **Audit the plastic in your garden:** Take a look at the plastic you already own and try to estimate its likely useful lifespan, should you decide to keep it, compared to its likely fate (and environmental impact) if you give it away, recycle it or otherwise offload it. Consider which are the things you love and use a lot? These are keepers, even if they're made of plastic. Make a list of items (or techniques) that you want to offload, replace or change, then prioritise ruthlessly. A useful guiding principle for this

prioritising might be to aim first for the low-hanging fruit, i.e. the changes that might have the biggest effect for the least effort. Or you could tackle the things that bother you most, since you'll probably be most motivated to change them. Take the top one to five priority items, no more. These are the things to focus your energy on. Forget the others on your list, for now.

2. **Reduce, reuse, recycle:** Where you can, reduce the new plastic you buy and use, for instance by buying less, planting less or switching to paper pots. Keep using the plastic items that are still functional and fit for purpose, or that can be reused for another purpose. Round up the materials you have decided you will no longer use and take them to your local garden centre if they operate a pots and trays recycling scheme. In Fife, Scotland, Growforth Nursery accepts trays and pots from retail customers at weekends and from wholesale customers via its collection scheme. They hope to expand this service to increase pot and tray recycling in Scotland substantially. In England and Wales, several members of the HTA horticulture trade body also operate pot and tray recycling services for their customers. Failing that, take your plastic things to your local refuse site to put into the most appropriate waste skip (although at the time of writing, many local authorities, over 80%, can't or won't recycle opaque plastic plant pots of any colour even if you take them directly to the tip, so the pots will go into the landfill skip or to an incinerator in many cases). This is, at least, responsible disposal: the plastic waste has a good chance of staying within the waste disposal site

where it is placed, rather than being blown or washed into a fragile environmental niche where it could do harm.

3. **Donate:** If the materials you no longer want are in good condition, you may be able to give them to local gardening groups, but most will be in the same position as you, overloaded with plastic (especially pots) and not in need of more. Where appropriate, you could offer your unwanted stash via sites such as Gumtree or Freecycle, or even in the old-fashioned way, by pinning an advert on a community noticeboard. If the stars align, your unwanted plastic goods could be handed on to someone who will use them for a little longer.

4. **Research** alternatives to the plastic things you buy and use most regularly and try to find local suppliers. Ask your existing suppliers whether they might be able to stock plastic-free options. See the list of suppliers at the end of this book and the products discussed in earlier chapters.

5. **Switch** to plastic-free products for one or two of your most frequently used items e.g. pots, where there is an easy to source option that you can buy or make without taking out a bank loan or spending several hours driving or surfing the web.

6. **Make a plan** for the more difficult changes and implement gradually, focusing on a small clutch of actions at a time.

7. **Review** market options regularly as new products may arrive that weren't available, affordable or of good quality last season.

8. **Repeat** this process. Return to your audit and work on the next priority, with a preference for the most

frequently used items and the easy wins that promise a good payoff for a modest investment of effort.

9. **Preserve** what you have. It may seem counter-intuitive to try to prolong the life of plastic things, but the more you can make something last, the longer it remains a useful possession as opposed to a potential piece of litter. This is really a case of reduce and reuse. Try to keep plastic items out of the sun: store them in a dark shed as UV light will make them brittle and they'll become unusable more quickly.

10. **Share information** about responsible recycling and disposal and great alternative products and techniques. If your municipal tip will accept coloured plastic plant pots and trays for recycling and or you have access to a rigid plastics recycling service, make use of it and let others know it is there. You can share these tips online via the hashtag, **#plasticfreegardening**

11

HABITS AND APPROACHES TO STAY PLASTIC-FREE

It's not what you do but the way that you do it.

- Buy less. Or buy fewer single-use plastic items (i.e. reduce).
- Buy more – of things that will last and be reused many times, and that can be recycled easily.
- Adopt a less-is-more approach to your garden: many of us tend to clutter our plot with too many plants, colours, textures and forms, despite our best intentions. But reducing the range of materials, colours and varieties can lead to a more unified design with a relaxing mood, giving you less upkeep to do and improving the overall look. Likewise, having fewer containers to tend to will reduce the work and maintenance you need to do as well as cutting down on plastic.
- Love the plot you've got. Working with the soil type, shade and local weather conditions and celebrating them by growing things that will thrive in your

unique microclimate will probably mean you need to bring in fewer products and materials. If you try to change your soil pH or bring in plants that are very tender and need lots of cossetting, you're likely to need more soil additives or plant protection such as tunnels and cloches (which may well involve plastic). Stick to plants that love the temperatures and pH of your part of the world and they won't need these extra props.

- Save seed: if you save at least some seed, you'll be less reliant on seed companies and the unwelcome surprise plastic layers sometimes found in seed packaging. Store your seed in jars or paper envelopes.
- Use mulches: to reduce weeds and water evaporation – so you'll need to use your watering can or hose less, and hopefully reduce the need for plastic weed suppressant membranes. Mulching materials to try include: spent mushroom compost, grass clippings, bark chips, newspaper or cardboard and garden compost (ideally hot-composted to reduce weed seed).
- Invest in fewer, better quality materials and clothing.
- Include plastic use as a criterion when trying to choose between suppliers for plants and garden sundries.
- Support suppliers that are trying to reduce their plastic or boost plastic reuse and recycling levels by giving them your custom where possible.
- Buy plants bare-rooted or buy as seed.
- Gather inspiration from books, magazines, TV programmes and websites like Pinterest to find creative ways to garden with less plastic.
- Propagation: try gradually switching the balance of

your plants to perennial vegetables, fruit and flowers rather than raising so many plants from seed or buying them anew in plastic pots every season. Perennial plants to try include: rhubarb, currant bushes, sea kale, asparagus, certain forms of kale, Babington leeks, buckler-leafed sorrel, oca, Welsh onions, Egyptian walking onions, wall rocket, rhubarb chard, globe and Jerusalem artichokes, garlic cress and the prolific self-seeders that can almost be treated like perennials e.g. nasturtiums and sweet cicely. For flowers, look to the new perennial planting style for inspiration on which varieties work well in your garden conditions, including the books of Piet Oudolf.

- Try vegetative propagation e.g. by cuttings and divisions, to increase your own stock of produce crops and ornamentals. Soft and hard wood cuttings, root cuttings, pegging, air layering and division can all give you plants for free and bypass plastic entirely. If you are yearning for plants you don't already have, it's worth asking if friends or neighbours grow it and whether it's a plant you can take cuttings (or collect seed) from at the right time of year. Most of your cuttings and divisions can be grown on in a nursery bed or in a wooden or clay pot or tray in sand-heavy mixes of compost.

- But it's also important to keep supporting our growers so buying from nurseries and garden centres should be something that continues to enhance your gardening life. As previously mentioned, it should become gradually easier now to buy new plants that don't come in pots made from non-recyclable plastic.

- Seedling propagation: seeds can be germinated in a

propagation bed, either in a greenhouse or tunnel, or outdoors, covered with glass panes for hardier varieties. Sowing in wooden seed trays or paper or terracotta pots in a cold frame or on a potting shed windowsill are other time-honoured ways to raise seedlings. For many varieties, the simple methods have yet to be bettered, e.g. paper pots on a ceramic or metal tray on the windowsill of a bright room.

- Community gardens: local groups may be able to teach you about sustainable gardening techniques including composting and may be able to help with swapping and lending of plants and seeds, tools and equipment.

- Consider modifying the crops you grow, perhaps limit the varieties to those that can be sown direct outdoors. It'll save you time and effort as well as avoiding the need for plastic pots altogether. This is a more radical suggestion, maybe, but its appeal is in its simplicity.

- Use your wheelbarrow more: bring it to the edge of a vegetable bed or flower border when weeding so you won't need a plastic trug or bucket. Bring it to the compost heap so you don't need to shovel compost into a bucket first. Or wheel your garden waste bin to wherever you're weeding – again, cutting out the middle step which might involve a plastic trug. But if for reasons of space, physical fitness or other considerations you do need to collecting weeds in a small plastic bucket or trug, don't worry. These can, in theory, be recycled. The tricky thing is getting your small load of domestic plastic into the incoming raw material stream for a nearby rigid plastics recycling plant.

PLASTIC-FREE HEROES: A SELECTION

- **Alluring Plants Nursery** – Uses biodegradable pots (coir and Vipots) or reused plastic pots and peat-free compost. Based on a Shropshire farm, offers pollen and nectar rich plants to sustain bees and butterflies. Pam's Pools, Underton, Near Bridgnorth, Shropshire,

WV16 6TY. Tel: 07747 574268 www.alluringplants.co.uk

- **Ban the Bead** – Information about avoiding microbeads. www.beatthemicrobead.org
- **Chillington Tools –** Traditionally made tools, ash and steel construction. Supply replacement heads and handles so you can repair and keep using favourite tools for longer. Crocodile House, Strawberry Lane, Willenhall, West Midlands, WV13 3RS, UK Tel: 01902 826 826 www.chillingtontoolsonline.co.uk
- **(The) Coastal Gardener** – Nursery on the Isle of Wight where the owners have decided not to buy in any new plastic pots and are going to trial biodegradable ones instead. While they'll continue to use the pots they have and those given by local contractors, they're looking at how to reduce plastic usage generally. Tel: 07977 550050 Fakenham Farm, Eddington Road, St Helens, Isle of Wight PO33 1XS www.thecoastalgardener.co.uk
- **(The) Edible Culture Nursery** in Faversham, Kent recently featured on BBC *Gardeners' World* programme, has committed to 'never letting a plastic pot leave the premises' and have stopped bringing any new plastic on site. Their beautiful, plastic-free, 'Fork Handles' shop is a shining example of what can be done. Everything is sold loose and then wrapped in paper or put into folding cardboard Posi Pots (www.posipots.co.uk) for transporting home. The plants can be planted out in the pots, which will rot away quickly. The Horticulture Unit, The Abbey School, London Rd, Faversham ME13 8RZ. Tel: 01795 537662 www.edibleculture.co.uk

- **Green Tones** – Online sustainable homeware shop that sells bamboo pots. www.greentones.co.uk
- **Growforth Ltd** – Recycling of pots and trays, mainly for garden centres but also for retail customers (weekends). Plans to expand this scheme to cover more of Scotland. South Pargillis, Cockluine Road, Hillend, Dunfermline, Fife, KY11 7HS. Tel: 01383 415555 www.growforth.co.uk
- **Kirton Farm Nurseries Ltd (the Hairy Pot Plant Company)** – Cottage garden plants and herbs, raised and supplied in biodegradable coir pots. They also supply wooden display boxes. Mainly wholesale, but you can buy Hairy Pot Company plants via any of the stockists listed on their website. Crawley, Winchester, Hampshire, SO21 2PJ. Tel: 01962 776493 www.kirtonfarm.co.uk
- **Nutscene** – A huge number of useful products that could replace plastic articles in your gardening life. The most famous is twine, made on original equipment from 1922 and available in an array of colours. But they also sell oak cane toppers, wooden dibbers and slate labels. Kingston Works, Kingston Place, Kingsmuir, By Forfar, Angus, DD8 2RG. Tel: 01307 468589 www.nutscene.com
- **Real Seeds** – Vegetable and herb seeds, changing some of their seed packets to paper from plastic for 2019. PO Box 18, Newport near Fishguard, Pembrokeshire SA65 0AA. Tel: 01239 821107 www.realseeds.co.uk
- **Scrumptious Gardens** – Central Scotland garden design and build partnership specialising in edible gardens, has a policy never to use plastic pots. Use

the Paperpot System for propagation.
www.scrumptiousgarden.com

- **Sea Spring Seeds** – Paper-wrapped seeds for a wide range of carefully trialled vegetables from this company in Dorset. A particular penchant for chillies. Sea Spring Farm, West Bexington, Dorchester, Dorset, DT2 9DD. Tel: 01308 897898. www.seaspringseeds.co.uk
- **Tiffanie Turner** – Paper flower artist, www. papelsf.com
- **Withypitts Dahlias** – Uses biodegradable pots for all stock. Turners Hill, West Sussex RH10 4SF. Tel: 0800 304 7124. www.withypitts-dahlias.co.uk
- **www.gardeningwithoutplastic.com** – Useful blog and website from garden writer Sally Nex.

13

CONCLUSION

It's such an interesting time to think about plastic and gardens. The world is beginning to wake up, as if from a bad dream, and recognise the dark side of our love for this flexible, shape-shifting material. At the same time, new research, legislation and product development is popping up everywhere. Momentous changes in public awareness have come about thanks, partly, to the Sir David Attenborough BBC One documentary, *Blue Planet II.* The distress calls we see in the news, regularly now, of coastal and riverside communities as well as wildlife conservation groups around the world who are feeling the brunt of the plastic tide's most damaging effects won't allow us to forget the problem. Arguably, it's a great time to reflect and make changes if you think you need to, because while some changes might not require any equipment or products, just a different technique or approach, other modifications will require alternative tools and sundries such as labels and pots. These are beginning to be more widely available, as are more plastics recycling schemes.

But it's not straightforward, with a dizzying storm of claim and counter claim made by branding wizards for the 'biodegradable', 'eco-friendly', 'plastic-free' even 'compostable' credentials of products and so many new things hitting the market at once. It's bewildering to say the least. Often the products badged with such claims to environmental superiority are made from materials whose extraction and processing have a deleterious effect on ecosystems as bad or worse than an equivalent plastic article. Worse still, it can be almost impossible for us to navigate these claims and know which brands and products to trust. For now, some plastic products may remain a better option than their proposed substitutes, when considered in the round, especially those made from recycled materials that can themselves be easily recycled. But the changes now underway should bring an ever-increasing choice of plastic-free products and methods to use in tending our patch of earth.

The information and suggestions in these pages are aimed at making it a little easier to navigate the often confusing path to plastic-free or sustainable, low-plastic gardening. Because this is a time of flux, the best ways to reduce plastic in our gardens will change over time. With this in mind, it'll help if we share any tips we discover that could help others trying to reduce their reliance on plastic. If you find helpful techniques, ideas and products not mentioned in this book, or that supersede the suggestions here, please do share them via social media using the hashtag #**plasticfreegardening** – or contact the Trellis team via the website or info@trellisscotland.org.uk and we'll gather and share the updates.

Happy gardening!

ACKNOWLEDGMENTS

We would like to express our sincere thanks to all the people who helped with suggestions, critiques of early drafts, new insights and encouragement: Jan Cameron, Jane Campbell, Jo Cook, Jean Gavin, Stan Green, Diana Robertson, Jenny Simpson, Sharon Watters, Joan Wilson, Claire Wingfield. With thanks to Sharon Watters for cover photography.

Keep in touch

Sign up to our mailing list to stay up to date with our work and future publications on the Plastic-free Gardener pages of our site: www.trellisscotland.org.uk/plasticfreegardener

If you'd like to share this book with other readers, book reviews posted on sites like Goodreads or on social media at @Trellis_Network (Twitter) or @TrellisScotland (Facebook) really help!

INDEX